Roanoke County Public Library
South County Library
6303 Merriman Road
Roanoke, VA 24018

W9-CJW-904

NO LONGER PROPERTY OF ROANOKE COUNTY PUBLIC LIBRARY

0 1197 0704160 2

FROGS AND TOADS
BREEDING AND KEEPING

W. P. Mara

Frogs and toads make wonderful pets, and most specimens can be obtained for reasonably low prices. Some, like the Red-eyed Treefrog, *Agalychnis callidryas*, that this sculpture is modeled after, are remarkably beautiful. Photo by W. P. Mara.

t.f.h.

NO LONGER PROPERTY OF ROANOKE COUNTY PUBLIC LIBRARY

© **1994 by T.F.H. Publications, Inc.**

Distributed in the UNITED STATES to the Pet Trade by T.F.H. Publications, Inc., One T.F.H. Plaza, Neptune City, NJ 07753; distributed in the UNITED STATES to the Bookstore and Library Trade by National Book Network, Inc. 4720 Boston Way, Lanham MD 20706; in CANADA to the Pet Trade by H & L Pet Supplies Inc., 27 Kingston Crescent, Kitchener, Ontario N2B 2T6; Rolf C. Hagen Ltd., 3225 Sartelon Street, Montreal 382 Quebec; in CANADA to the Book Trade by Macmillan of Canada (A Division of Canada Publishing Corporation), 164 Commander Boulevard, Agincourt, Ontario M1S 3C7; in ENGLAND by T.F.H. Publications, PO Box 15, Waterlooville PO7 6BQ; in AUSTRALIA AND THE SOUTH PACIFIC by T.F.H. (Australia), Pty. Ltd., Box 149, Brookvale 2100 N.S.W., Australia; in NEW ZEALAND by Brooklands Aquarium Ltd. 5 McGiven Drive, New Plymouth, RD1 New Zealand; in Japan by T.F.H. Publications, Japan—Jiro Tsuda, 10-12-3 Ohjidai, Sakura, Chiba 285, Japan; in SOUTH AFRICA by Multipet Pty. Ltd., P.O. Box 35347, Northway, 4065, South Africa. Published by T.F.H. Publications, Inc.
MANUFACTURED IN THE UNITED STATES OF AMERICA
BY T.F.H. PUBLICATIONS, INC.

TABLE OF CONTENTS

Author's Dedication

A Short Story...

For a child, making contact with the people you look up to is a pretty big deal. When I first started getting involved in the hobby of herpetoculture, I remember how badly I wanted to make friends with all the "big names" in my fun new field of interest.

Between the initial writing of this book and its eventual publication, I received a letter from a little girl in Ohio who asked me for some advice on how to go about obtaining salamanders. She mentioned that she had a particular fondness for Marbled Salamanders, so I sent her an adult pair I happened to have at the time.

From that point on, we were friends, writing back and forth every so often, she showing her bubbling enthusiasm with every sentence, and I trying my best to help her with her endeavors. What impressed me most about her was her intense love for all amphibians. In the United States, reptiles far outweigh them in terms of popularity, and yet this wonderful child had the insight to realize what fascinating creatures frogs, toads, salamanders, and all the rest of the amphibian clan could really be.

And so, I thought I would dedicate not only a single page but a whole book to my bright young friend. I have always set my sights on animals that most people overlook, and it thrilled me to meet another who shared this most rewarding perspective.

So, this one is for you, Melissa, with my eternal and most sincere admiration.

Keep at it.

Introduction

So, you've decided to keep a frog or a toad as a pet, have you? Well, you've made a good choice, both in books and pets. Frogs and toads can be among the most rewarding of all animals, with their varied good looks and amusing habits, but you before you get too deeply involved in them you should first learn their basics, and that's where this guide comes in useful.

This book was specifically designed with you, the dilettante, in mind. It has been tailor-made to answer your every question, remove your every worry, and supply you with every bit of data you'll need to mold a strong, dependable foundation for your newly acquired interest. It was created for the specific purpose of arming the budding hobbyist with enough precise information to make every future undertaking as enjoyable, enduring, and as safe (for both you and the animals) as possible. I have endeavored to make the facts clear and unmistakable, with little room for error, because those very same errors could one day mean the life or death of one of your pets, and the latter is not part of our menu. It is simply not a goal we wish to achieve.

So with all this in mind, I suggest you now read on and let each page take you one step closer to being the most competent frog and toad keeper you can be.

W. P. Mara

One of the best things about frogs and toads is that most of them can be maintained on a diet of small insects, most of which can be obtained with a minimum of effort. Even a young child could responsibly care for a frog or a toad. Photo of a *Polypedates leucomystax*, by Paul Freed.

Red-eyed Treefrogs, *Agalychnis callidryas*, are commercially available and not too difficult to maintain in captivity. They eat crickets and prefer setups with plenty of leaf cover. Photo by David Dube.

The Basics

Millions and millions of years ago, in a dark, murky swamp somewhere, a small, fish-like creature peered its head out of the water and squirmed up onto dry land. Perhaps this happened because the community it lived in was becoming too crowded, or maybe the ponds and streams were beginning to dry up, leaving it no other choice.

Either way, that first bold step was also the first step toward the evolution of frogs and toads, and sparked off a transformation process that still, interestingly enough, continues today.

It all began about 225 million years ago during a time in the earth's history known as the Triassic Period. That is when, the experts say, the first "frog-like" creatures appeared. Of course, they did not look the same as they do now; they had larger tails, cruder lungs, and poorly developed legs. They evolved, as indeed many other creatures did, from certain types of fish, and were forced onto dry land by a wide variety of violent ecological events, two of which have already been suggested.

As the centuries passed, some of these early amphibians began adapting to terrestrial life

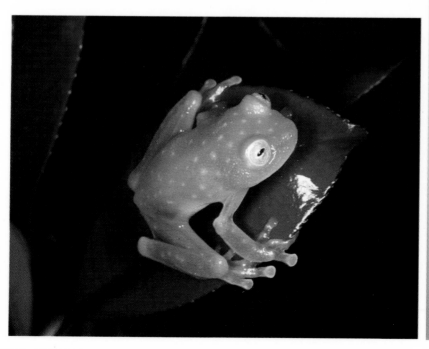

Frogs have been around a long time—over 200 million years, according to the experts. They evolved from fishes that were forced onto land when their waters became inhabitable. Photo of a South American Glass Frog, *Centrolenella fleischmanni*, by Paul Freed.

In terms of color and pattern, many frogs and toads vary greatly even within the same species. These two pretty little frogs, for example, appear fairly different, particularly in dorsal pattern, and yet they both are Clown Tree Frogs, *Hyla leucophyllata*. Photo by Paul Freed.

with stunning progress. Complete respiratory systems replaced gills, dexterity of movement improved, and acceptable dietary substitutes were found and utilized. They learned to adapt, and then thrive, in a setting that only a few eras before would have proved lethal. Now, it would be called home.

others, and vice-versa, but for the most part they all fit into the generally accepted spirit of the word.

One question that gets asked quite often is, "what's the difference between a frog and a toad?" To put it quite simply, not a whole lot. They are in fact closely akin to one another,

One fascinating characteristic of many anurans is bright coloration. In many cases, this tells predators that the frog or toad in question may have toxic skin secretions and should be avoided. Shown is a Golden Mantella, *Mantella aurantiaca*, from Madagascar. Photo by Isabelle Francais.

The exact meaning of the word "amphibious," according to any standard dictionary is, "to be able to live both on land and in water." Indeed, this describes our small friends quite accurately. Of course, some amphibians are more dependent on water than

except perhaps that the frog is usually more aquatic, and the toad a bit "wartier." Both terms originated in Britain many, many years ago based on each creature's external texture. "Frog" means wet or slimy, and "toad" means dry.

The actual hobby of

A frog that smiles? That is often the sentiment expressed by people seeing the immensely popular White's Tree Frog, *Litoria caerulea*, for the first time. A native of Australia and New Guinea, it eats well, can live in a variety of surroundings, and responds well to human company. Photo by Isabelle Francais.

Among the most intriguing, and undoubtedly the most attractive, of all anurans are the poison frogs, family Dendrobatidae. Also known as the "poison arrow" or "poison dart" frogs, many species do well in the home, provided, of course, you can furnish them with the correct food items (some of which are very small). Photo of the Harlequin Poison Frog, *Dendrobates histrionicus*, by Isabelle Francais, courtesy of Eric Anderson.

keeping frogs and toads is part of something known as *herpetoculture*, or, more specifically, *amphibioculture*. A loose definition of the former word is, "the keeping and propagation of reptiles and amphibians," the second word referring particularly to just the amphibians. The mere meaning of the first word encompasses quite a bit,

to keep, admire, touch, and study, and without a doubt some of the most fascinating organisms on this earth.

As far as anyone can tell, the actual practice of keeping frogs and toads goes back as far as the late 1700's, when many of the earliest herpetologists housed them for scientific study. I guess you couldn't really call these

Note the visible internal organs in this South American Glass Frog, *Centrolenella fleischmanni.* It should be obvious from this photo (by Isabelle Francais) how this frog got its common name—you can see right through it!

as you can probably tell, for not only are frogs and toads a part of the herpetological kingdom, but also snakes, turtles, iguanas, alligators, crocodiles, caimans, newts, sirens, mudpuppies, salamanders, and skinks, plus a few others. They are all wonderful animals

early situations part of the "hobby" per se, but there is little doubt that those who were involved probably still felt the same tangible intrigue that grips most of us today. Even I, after many years of keeping, hunting, photographing, breeding, taming, training, and writing about so many different members of the herp community, can still get those same initial pangs of excitement when I see a new specimen for the first time. Even common examples that I have come across already inspire some kind of odd thrill. Frogs and toads, not to mention all the others, are just simply that way. My guess is

the head. If it weren't for the hard work and tireless dedication of a man by the name of Raymond Ditmars, chances are very good that same reaction would probably still be in vogue today. Ditmars was the first person to ever "go public" with his feelings about herptiles and spent basically his entire life studying and writing

The Cuban Treefrog, *Osteopilus septentrionalis*, is a highly affordable and very hardy captive, thriving on a diet of vitamin-enriched crickets and mealworms. It is an excellent "starter" frog for anyone interested in this angle of herpetoculture. Photo by Isabelle Francais.

that's how its always been, since this fantastic hobby first began.

But, turning herpetoculture into a popular pastime wasn't easy. For years anyone who expressed an interest in such bizarre creatures was greeted with one eyebrow raised and a sympathetic shaking of

about them. His books and papers were both educative and amusing, and he himself, as reptile curator of the Bronx Zoo, became quite a celebrity. His name became synonymous with these beautiful but sometimes terribly misunderstood creatures, and thus he almost single-handedly

Perhaps the most endearing characteristic of the Red-eyed Treefrog, *Agalychnis callidryas*, is its striking yet simple coloration. Here, you can clearly see the reds, yellows, and beautiful blues, all of which make the animal look more like a child's toy than a living creature. Photo by Isabelle Francais.

The Eyelash Frog, *Ceratobatrachus guentheri*, is a native of the Solomon Islands and is not, as many people suspect, that closely related to the horned frogs of the genus *Ceratophrys*. It also is not difficult to care for. Photo by Isabelle Francais.

delivered the birth of herpetoculture as an acceptable domestic undertaking, then raised it into infancy so it could be orphaned off to such fine minds as Laurence Klauber, Frank Nelson Blanchard, Henry S. Fitch, and of course, the well-known Dr. Roger Conant.

Generally speaking, the and their backbones are quite small (only eight vertebrae). In particular, frogs are, as I mentioned before, the more aquatic of the two, thus their skin is generally smoother, slimier, shinier, and more sleek. They have been modified through the ages to adapt equally as well to water as on land, but they will never stray far from a

As many frogs grow older, their colors and patterns change. This Tomato Frog, *Dyscophus guineti*, for example, will be uniformly orange in adulthood. Photo by Paul Freed.

frog and the toad can best be described in visual terms as small creatures, with flat heads, striking eyes, four legs (long and usually webbed on the rear and short but powerful and dexterous in the front), and an endless variety of eye-catching dorsal color variations. As adults, they have no tails brook or a stream, most of them springing out and plunging under the surface at the first sign of trouble.

Toads on the other hand have dry, mottled skin, with a whole array of warts, bumps, and other distinct dermal interruptions that give them a slightly prehistoric appearance. In fact, if it were not for their meager sizes they would probably look quite frightening. They are for the most part exclusive to the land, although always near water, but hardly ever in use of it. They prefer drier, sandier domain, but will usually settle down in the more moist sections of these areas anyway.

company of others, and will favor these conditions at every opportunity. Surprisingly enough, however, they still adapt very well to captivity, and that is of course good news for you, the newly ordained hobbyist. Unlike so many other members of the herpetological circle (like the alligator or the cobra), frogs and toads

Notice the heavy warting on this Central American Treefrog, *Phrynohyas venulosus*. Wartiness usually is a characteristic of anurans referred to as "toads." This specimen, incidentally, is a patternless morph of a normally much more decorative animal. Photo by Paul Freed.

Both the frog and the toad are somewhat secretive, like most reptiles or amphibians who prefer the confines of solitude to the extroverted amenities that go with the

will adapt to almost any situation, whether it be in someone's outdoor pond or a 20-gallon glass aquarium, and then thrive for years, given proper care.

Most toads prefer drier surroundings than frogs do. Many, in fact, can be kept in desert-type setups. You should, however, know as much about your own animal's natural habitat as possible before you follow such a general rule. Photo of a little Garman's Toad, *Bufo garmani,* resting atop a Marine Toad, *Bufo marinus*, by Isabelle Francais.

Housing Your Pet

In this chapter, we will discuss and examine all the ramifications that go with keeping your new frog or toad in an artificial environment that is both practical and beneficial to you and your small friend. To begin with, let's review each type of setup individually.

VARIOUS SETUPS

As with anything, there is more than one way to house a frog or a toad. Ideally speaking, this depends almost entirely on its natural habitat.

Below is a quick rundown of each of the four standard setups:

1) The Aquatic Tank. Quite simply, a fishtank with a frog in it; no land masses required. In many ways, the aquatic tank is the simplest to start, and to maintain. For one, your choice of cage bedding is virtually made for you (rocks or sand). Secondly, heating and filtration are a virtual cinch. Finally, humidity (a very important factor) is of no concern at all. Also, there are so many pet stores, societies, and publications, designed to aid the rapid advancement of the aquarium hobby

Opposite Page: Many of the walking toads, like this *Mecanophryniscus stelzneri,* while simply colored on the back, have striking belly patterns. Photo by Isabelle Francais.

For the keeping of smaller anurans, you can purchase a small, hexagonal tank and put it right in your bedroom or on your desk. Most pet shops carry these. Photo courtesy of Hagen.

Small plastic tanks are not only good for keeping smaller frogs and toads, they can also be used to transport them from place to place or as holding quarters while their main tanks are being cleaned. Photo courtesy of Hagen.

that you will certainly never be at a loss for contemporary information sources.

2) The Terrestrial Tank. Usually reserved for toads, but many frogs benefit from it as well. Basically nothing more than a simple terrarium with a small water supply. The keeper of a terrestrial tank has a wide variety of plants, rocks, and substrates (another name for cage beddings) at their disposal. They can be, and should be, designed very attractively. This may require a little extra work, but the results are unprecedented.

3) The "Half and Half." The most common anuran tank. A large body of water plus a large body of land. Such tanks are often

Lighted hoods work well with frogs and toads, and the fliptop lid that many of these feature makes it easy for a keeper to drop infood items. Photo courtesy of Hagen.

referred to as paludariums or aquaterrariums. If one really takes the time they can manage a setup of this kind that is both imminently practical and visually breathtaking.

4) The Arboreal Tank. Arboreal simply means tree-dwelling. Peepers, treefrogs, etc., live in these tanks. One must acquire special enclosures (extra high) if they want to keep an arboreal anuran happy.

this, we will examine each facet separately.

Tanks
Unlike other herps, frogs and toads cannot generally survive in homemade tanks. This is not to say that you don't have the skills necessary to give them competitive living quarters, but unlike, say, snakes, who do fairly well in a large wood and chicken wire container, frogs and toads need more "water-friendly" surroundings;

Plastic containers come in a variety of shapes and sizes, and can be found for sale in many pet shops. One of the nicest aspects of using these containers is that they are easy to manipulate during cleaning time. Photo courtesy of Hagen.

It's worth it though, because some of the most attractive frogs and toads in the world fall into this category.

From this basic list you should have no trouble assimilating which type of setup your animal or animals will need. Now, you should learn how to set it up. In order to do

something wood is not generally known for.

If you're thinking about going to the considerable trouble of learning how to cut your own glass and use your own sealant, let me tell you from experience that it's just not worth it. Realistically speaking, you will probably spend more time

Needless to say, you probably shouldn't house this many Green Treefrogs, *Hyla cinerea*, in the same tank at the same time. One of the central problems with overcrowding is the competition for food—some frogs will grow quite fat while others will die of starvation. Neither condition is preferable. Photo by Isabelle Francais, courtesy of Tom Crutchfield.

and money this way than if you just went out and bought yourself a standard factory-made glass tank in the first place.

So where can you go to get these glass tanks, or *aquariums* (and even *vivariums*), as they are commonly called? In a pet store, of course. No doubt you've seen them there before, stacked so high on

(both on land and in water). For the last three, the tank itself is not really so much the question (as long as it's water-tight), but for the first you will need one that is somewhat taller than usual. Of course, there are plenty available, so acquiring one will not be a problem.

Size is an important consideration here too.

Frogs with developmental anomalies, like this five-legged Marine Toad, *Bufo marinus,* probably should be housed alone because many have trouble competing for food. Photo by Isabelle Francais.

the shelves wrapped in cardboard protector sheets? Which one are you going to buy? This depends on the animal in question. What kind of frog or toad is it? Again, there are four types: arboreal (tree-dwelling), aquatic (always in water), terrestrial (always on land), and half & half

Basically, most frogs and toads are quite small. Even some of the larger commercial types (like the Colorado River Toad, *Bufo alvarius,* for example) can live quite comfortably in a 20-gallon setting. And, naturally, the more frogs and/or toads you have, the more space you'll need.

Poison frogs, like this stunning Blue Poison Frog, *Dendrobates azureus*, should only be housed with others of their kind. Frogs and toads with high toxicity are definitely dangerous to other species. Photo by Isabelle Francais.

The Colorado River Toad, *Bufo alvarius*, is a good example of a frog that should be kept alone—it can grow very large (up to 7 in/ 17.9 cm) and wouldn't think twice before gulping down another, smaller member of its order (or any other for that matter). Photo by J. W. Church.

For the most part, anything under 3 in/7.6 cm can live well in a 10-gallon tank, and anything larger will require a 20 or even a 30. For every two more you acquire, increase your tank size 5 to 10 gallons. That is a fairly reliable rule of thumb and should be followed. Most frogs and toads don't really mind mildly cramped quarters once they get used to them, but there is a limit.

Tank Tops

To indulge in this next topic seems almost impudent. After all, What kind of rules and regulations could possibly apply to something as basic as putting a top on a tank?

In truth there aren't that many, but there are a few. The worst part of it is, they are subtle. The kind of small, easy-to-miss-until-something-has-gone-wrong type of details that many people learn about the hard way (herpetoculture is a great host for irritants like this, but if you're careful you can learn to avoid them).

For starters, ventilation is a key issue. If you feel the openings in the top are too large for security purposes and suspect

some of your pets might try wandering off, cover them over with some soft screening (as the harder stuff may prove too abrasive, especially for those types who always leap toward the roof of their tanks hoping to pop the lids off). Along similar

Bombina orientalis, due to a poorly situated top. You'd be amazed how Houdini-like amphibians can be.

Finally, remember that you are going to be adding some light on your subjects, so leave space for that.

Screen covers are good for use with frogs and toads, but with species that require a great amount of humidity, you may have to add a sheet of clear plastic wrap over the tank opening before putting these tops on. Beyond that, they are practical, attractive, and quite affordable. Check with your local pet shop. Photo courtesy of Four Paws.

lines, don't let *too much* air get into the tank of any frog or toad that needs moisture, because draftiness will dry everything up very quickly. Dry amphibians that should be wet will die in a short space of time.

And of course, keep the tops secure. Since frogs and toads aren't know for their strength this may sound a bit exaggerated, but then that's what I used to think until I lost a prized Firebelly Toad,

Lighting

Unlike turtles and lizards, frogs and toads are not in dire need of something called *full-spectrum light*. The purpose of such lighting in the first place is to allow the animal's body to produce vitamin D_3.

Our small amphibian friends acquire their D_3 through other means, one of which is their diet, so only ordinary light is required (although it should be pointed out that

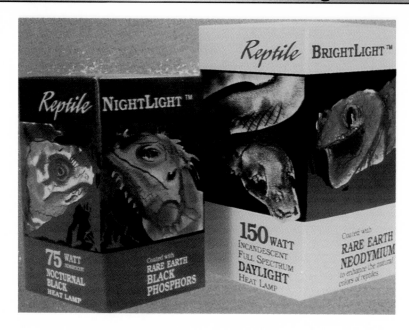

Providing your anurans with the correct photoperiod (day/night cycle) is an important consideration. There are a number of bulbs designed to help you meet this need. Photo courtesy of Energy Savers.

Beyond the correct light cycle, frogs and toads need the right kind of light as well. While many of them do not *require* full-spectrum lighting, a lot of keepers claim providing it makes their captives more healthy and improves breeding results. Photo courtesy of Energy Savers.

full-spectrum light, provided via a special full-spectrum bulb that you can purchase at many pet stores, will not do them any harm as long as the exposure is kept to about four or five hours per day).

Although many frogs and toads are nocturnal, they do need some light because it tells them what time of year it is just as the sun would if they were in nature. A good *photoperiod*, as it is called, should last around 12 hours a day. Don't use a bulb that shines too bright or you may damage their vision; at the very least you will have pets that hide all the time, and that is of course not very enjoyable for the keeper.

Humidity

In order to survive, your pets will need moisture. That does not mean you should just provide a waterbowl thinking they will simply dive into it when they feel dry; they

You really only should handle your frogs and toads when absolutely necessary. The fact is, most frogs and toads don't take kindly to the human touch. Photo by isabelle Francais.

Horned frogs of the genus *Ceratophrys* can be housed together when they are young, but as they grow they should be kept solitarily. This is a particularly voracious group that has a reputation for cannibalism (and love human fingers too). Photo by Isabelle Francais.

In order to retain moisture in a frog or toad's substrate, add in a little vermiculite. Vermiculite is a moisture-retaining product used mostly in the horticultural field. It can be bought in bags at most any garden center and is quite inexpensive. Photo by W. P. Mara

need moisture in the air as well.

If you have a basic North American frog or toad, you are somewhat fortunate. They do not need nearly as much humidity as most of the tropical and neo-tropical species do. In cases like this, you can do one of a few things:

1) Add and moisten a small layer of something called *vermiculite* (a water-retaining product

Providing moisture for your anurans never should be a problem. The simplest method is to use a pump-spray bottle. You should mist the tank every few days, holding the moisture in by stretching a piece of clear plastic wrap over the tank's opening, then poking a few tiny holes in the wrap with a pin so as to permit air circulation. Shown is a Red-eyed Treefrog, *Agalychnis callidryas*, perched on a bottle pump. Photo by Isabelle Francais.

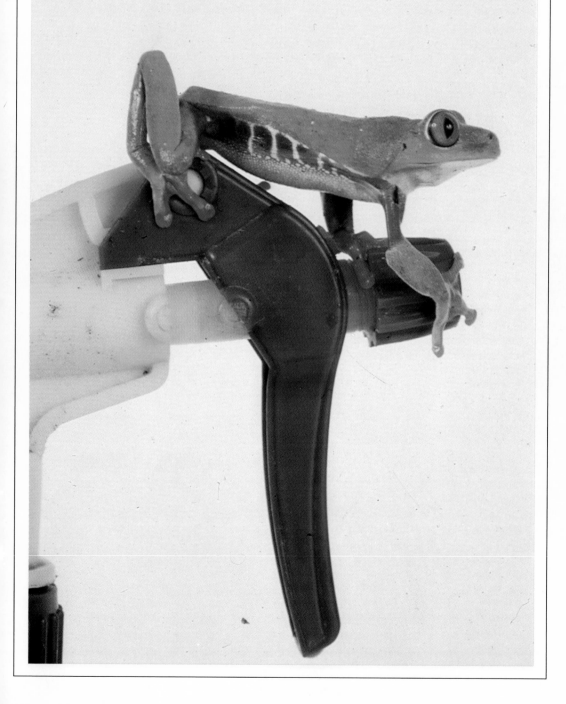

By placing an air-pumped airstone into the water body of an anuran's enclosure, you will provide better air circulation and increased humidity. Photo courtesy of Hagen.

found in any garden store) to the bottom of the tank before you spread on the regular substrate. This should suffice for at least a few days, and then you can methodically add more water as time goes by.

2) Try using a fine-mist spray bottle about once a day on the inside walls of the tank and perhaps just a touch on the bedding. This should yield the same results.

3) If you have live plants, spray them as well. They will hold moisture for quite some time, and chances are the animals will spend a lot of time on or around them. You can even spray the decorations and artificial plants too, although this is, of course, not as effective.

4) Finally, if you feel like going to a small amount of expense and trouble, you can place an airstone in the water. The oxygen rising up via the bubbles will also aid the moisturizing process.

For the most part, the "magic humidity number" is 60 %. Of course it doesn't have to be exactly that, but it should be close. Experiment with your tank for a few days. Take readings, try different things; eventually, you'll get it.

Heat emitters can be used to provide warmth in any herptile setup, but be careful you don't place the emitter *too* close, or the animals may not be able to get away from the heat when they wish to cool off. Many pet shops carry heat emitters. Photo courtesy of Zoo Med.

Heating

Here's an important issue: keeping the tanks warm. How do you do it? Do you warm just the water? Just the land? Both?

The last answer is correct, but only to a limited extent. Again, you must keep your subject's natural habitat in mind. If it's a tropical native then it will need high heat

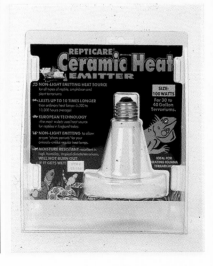

One good way of providing moisture for your frogs and toads is to moisten their substrate. Failing to do this would almost certainly mean death for many species. Photo by Isabelle Francais, courtesy of Bill and Marcia Brant.

It is always a good idea to keep a close eye on your anurans' ambient temperature. This can be done easily enough by purchasing a reliable thermometer. Photo courtesy of Hagen.

(about 80°F/26°C) all year long. If its used to a more shifting climate then 75°F/24°C is fine. But the question is, how?

Warming the Water

To warm any body of water, no matter what size, there are a few items on the commercial market at your disposal. The first one is the simple, thermostat-controlled, glass tube heater that attaches to the top of the tank and extends downward. These are perfectly reliable, and fairly inexpensive, but they have one fault: they need a high water level (which is rarely necessary for frogs and toads) in order to function properly. This will cause you to fill your tank up so much

there will be almost no room left for land masses, and that simply won't do. For aquatic setups they're ideal, but for the others they're not.

The other choice you have is the fully submersible heater, which

An easy way to warm tank water is to use a fully submersible heater. These come in a number of sizes and wattages and can be purchased at most pet shops. Photo courtesy of Hagen.

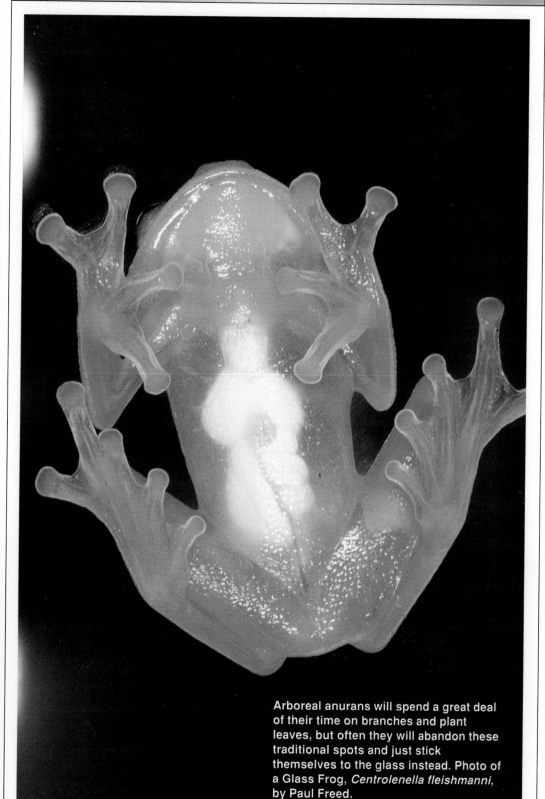

Arboreal anurans will spend a great deal of their time on branches and plant leaves, but often they will abandon these traditional spots and just stick themselves to the glass instead. Photo of a Glass Frog, *Centrolenella fleishmanni*, by Paul Freed.

is highly recommended. These also have complete thermostat control, plus they are dependable, long-lasting, and very efficient. The only problem here is they may cost a little more (although not much more), but in the long run they are definitely worth it. They usually come with a special plastic holder with two suction cups for easy placement, and the cords are heavily coated so none of your amphibs will run the risk of electrocution. One thing to beware of though: make sure the exit hole for the power line is closed up tight. Many a treefrog has crawled up and out of their tanks because of these cords.

Warming the Air

Now that you can heat the water, you must then heat the enclosure. This is also not particularly

Under-tank heating pads are a sensible option for creating tank warmth. They will warm only a certain section of the floor, which the captives can move onto or away from whenever they choose. Photo courtesy of Zoo Med.

difficult. These are the best options at your disposal:

1) The Ceramic Heater. Without question, the finest, most competent method of heating if you have more than a few setups is the ceramic heater, Not only is it efficient, but it's highly economical as well. Compared to other types of electric heaters, these will cost only about half as much to run, and probably even have a lower price tag to begin with. Simply place it in the room, set the thermostat, and that's it. Perhaps the only real flaw is, if your pets have heated water as well then this does not give them much of an opportunity to escape the heat when the urge takes them. One simple solution is to keep the water a bit cooler, but if you don't want to do that, then try—

2) The Heating Pad. A few companies are now producing a heating pad much in the same spirit of the famed "hot rock," but with the opportunity to heat the tank by placing the item on the outside rather than inside. Your pets need a place where they can go to

Plants with large leaves are a must in almost any anuran tank, especially those containing arboreal species. The leaves provide hiding places, which the frogs and toads need or else they will become highly stressed. Photo of a Spotted Treefrog, *Hyla punctata*, by Paul Freed.

One of the most attractive (and yet, sadly, commercially unavailable) hylids must be this striking Giraffe Treefrog, *Hyla favosa*, from South America. Such a frog would need a great degree of plant cover and a fairly high humidity/moisture level. Photo by Paul Freed.

warm up, but then leave it behind when they want to cool down. Heating their entire surround is not always such a good idea. This solves that problem, but you will have to use one with every tank.

3) The Heat Lamp. Another consideration to the problem, these

quarters with living creatures they get the urge to leap onto it, thus sustaining some mild burns in the process. Surprisingly enough, this doesn't really happen that often, but it's not a risk you should prefer to take. If you really want to use a heat lamp, cut

For terrestrial anuran species, a substrate of pine bark mulch is reasonable. Be sure to moisten it, however, and watch for fungal development. Mulch can be purchased in large bags and should be replaced at least once every ten days. Photo by Isabelle Francais, courtesy of Joe Fauci.

are commonly seen devices that consist of nothing more than a socket, sometimes a large aluminum hood, and a very hot bulb. They are quite reliable and reasonably low-priced, but if you intend to place the bulb directly in the tank, the top will have to be customized to house it. Sometimes when a bulb is put into close

a large hole in the top, cover it with wire cloth, and let the rays emanate from there, then add a hiding place out of rocks or wood or whatever so your captives can retreat to it when seeking shade.

As you can probably tell, the issue of heating methods is very much a personal affair, and your final actions will of course be based solely on your

Painted Mantella, *Mantella cowani*. Photo by Paul Freed.

own decision. Each method outlined above is perfectly feasible, so at least you have some choices. Keep in mind that air temperatures in the wild usually decrease as each day begins to die down. It would be wise on your part to obtain a small timer device so you can accurately recreate this process on a day-to-day basis. If you're keeping your specimens active in the winter and fear the temperature will go too low, you may have to actually readjust the thermostat every evening. If you're planning on eventually trying to breed your stock, then natural climate simulation becomes essential.

SUBSTRATES

As you may have noticed in the past, there are many different types

Malayan Leopard Frog, *Rana signata*. Photo by Paul Freed.

Red-legged
Walking
Frog,
*Kassina
maculata.*
Photo by
Paul Freed.

of cage beddings you can choose to cover the bottom of your tank. Of course, if you possess something totally aquatic like the African Clawed Frog, *Xenopus laevis,* (which has become an immensely popular hobby item in the last decade or so), then you really have no choice but to use gravel or sand.

But if this is not the case, then you have a few options at your disposal. Common potting soil is one, and not a bad one

Black-
legged
Poison
Frog,
*Phyllobates
bicolor.*
Photo by
Isabelle
Francais,
courtesy of
Eric
Anderson.

either. It's cheap, disposable, easy to obtain, perfectly natural, easy to keep moist, and you can add plants to it. By doing this you'll eventually have an actual terrarium with a few frogs and toads thrown in rather than the other way around; and your pets will love it. The only point you have to remember with soil is that the water supply must be kept well-separated from it or it will end up being more mud than anything else.

If the animal you have requires a slightly drier surrounding (like many of the toads), then sand is a good choice to consider. This is also fairly inexpensive and can be somewhat attractive too. With a few rocks and maybe some artificial plants thrown in, you could have a very nice display. Of course, keeping the water separate holds true here as well.

Finally, plain old gravel is just as good as it has always been. The advantages: a wide variety of colors and sizes, reusability, easy to clean, etc. Of course, every now and then your small friend may accidentally gulp one down, but this does not seem to bother them too much. In most cases the stones will just pass right through. When your diet consists almost exclusively of things you lick up off the ground, chances are you might sometimes get a little extra bonus with your meal. In the wild it probably happens quite often.

FILTRATION

Some people like to give their frogs and toads a nice big home, and of course there's nothing wrong with this. But the plain fact is, the more

room you afford them the more work it will be for you to keep it clean.

If you have three small peepers in a 20-gallon tank and the water area is small, then cleaning it out every week or so is not a major issue.

If, on the other hand,

In some ways, artificial plants are superior to live plants. For one, they do not have to be cared for in the culturing sense. Also, they can be washed and used over and over. Finally, they will not snap from an anuran's weight. There are many artificial plant varieties available at pet shops. Photo courtesy of Hagen.

When dealing with highly aquatic anurans, be sure to get yourself a reliable filter. This will not only save you the trouble of cleaning the tank every few days, but it will also make the environment generally safer for the captives. Photo courtesy of Hagen.

you have five large Bullfrogs, *Rana catesbeiana*, in a 55–or 100-gallon tank, and their "pond" is a foot deep, cleaning it every other day just might get a little irritating. Thus, the need for filtration arises.

There are three methods to what is called "active"

eventually, but this will certainly decrease the amount of times it has to be done. Change the cotton regularly and you will have no problems.

If you have gone to the trouble of furnishing your pets with a body of water even larger than that, an undergravel filter might be

filtration, which means quite simply, filtration that is active 24 hours a day.

The first is the standard corner box filter, which most everyone can hear in the pet stores bubbling away faithfully among the rows of 10-gallon tanks. If your frog or toad's water level is more than 4 in/ 10.1 cm deep but not over 20 gallons in content, then these will suffice. Of course, the water will have to be changed

nice. You can even use these in smaller quarters, and they really are quite efficient. For further details consult a good aquarium guide or contact your local pet shop and go from there.

Lastly, if you have a really big tank and think you can stand the noise, an external box filter will do the job quite well. External box filters are the heavy-duty units that hook over the rim of the tank with a suction tube

Most of the poison frogs, family Dendrobatidae, are highly terrestrial, so it won't be necessary to provide them with a large water body. Photo of three **Strawberry Poison Frogs**, *Dendrobates pumilio*, by Isabelle Francais.

extending down into the water, and either another tube or a simple opening for the return water a few inches to the right or left.

The problem with the noise is, sometimes there might be as much as a full foot of distance between the surface of the water and the top of the tank. Since these filters can only attach to the rims, the return stream will have to fall that distance to re-enter the pool. If you have a long outlet tube this may not be a problem, but if you don't (which is normally the case), then you may be in for some noisy aquatic effects.

One solution to this problem is to build up a small rock quarry directly under the stream thus creating a nice "trickle-down" waterfall-type effect. This also adds to the natural feel of your setup, and can be very attractive. The animals love it too. There will still be a small degree of "piddling" noises as the drops hit the pond surface, but it will be considerably less then the preceding noise and consequently much more tolerable.

LIVE PLANTS

When you consider the delicate ecology of the world around us, you begin to appreciate the realization that every living thing plays a special part in the makeup of the overall picture. When scientists talk about the "balance of nature," they

Mexican Treefrog, *Pachymedusa dacnicolor.* **Photo by Paul Freed.**

Malagasy Treefrog, *Boophis microtympanum*, from south-central Madagascar. Photo by Paul Freed.

mean it. We are all, in one way or another, dependent on other living organisms to some degree, and plants, as many of us know, play a crucial role.

If you decide to stock your tank's decor with artificial foliage, you are certainly not running the risk of doing your pets any harm. But if, on the other hand, you're thinking of having a go with some real ones, then I applaud you! Live plants are not only beautiful to the eye, they are also beneficial to the creatures that surround them.

So, which plants are the right ones and where can they be found? Those were two questions that plagued me when I first started setting up amphibian enclosures. Many guides tell you live plants are the ideal choice, but then don't tell you which ones to choose!

If you have a fully aquatic tank, then your best bets are plants like *Hygrophila difformis*, a handsome, hardy species with white-undersided leaves, *Anubias lanceolata*, a small, attractive, slow-grower, and maybe even a *Cabomba caroliniana*, a bushy plant that grows relatively fast but can sometimes be difficult to care for; it is very attractive and fills up dead space quite nicely. These all are usually available pet stores, and not terribly expensive.

If your vivarium is semi-

This is *Hygrophila difformis*, often referred to as a "temple plant." It is handsome, hardy, and would do well in most any anuran setup. Photo by B. Gieger.

terrestrial, then you have an enormous supply of foliage at your disposal. Because of this, it seems almost pointless to try and list any of them here. Suffice it to say all you really need to do is pay a visit to your local garden center and start choosing. Grab a guide on basic plant care while you're at it so your stock is well-maintained. Who knows? You may find yourself becoming an amateur horticulturist as well.

CAGE DECOR

Regardless of how far down on the priority ladder the subject of cage decor may seem, there certainly are a lot of people who dedicate much of their time and strength to it. Obviously, something like this is not half as important as proper dieting or heat control, yet it's an aspect of the hobby that fascinates many.

The appeal is really not so hard to figure out— nothing seems more pleasing to the eye than a nicely arranged, natural-looking aquarium with a few genuine floral representatives thrown in. To actually feel like you've captured a small block of true nature and imported it into your own home is a very addictive sensation.

What better way to improve upon that undertaking than to make your pets' tank look as real as possible? Some gravel and a waterbowl is all fine and well, but throw in a few rocks, a couple of plants, and a nice piece of driftwood, and all of a sudden you've

Anubias lanceolata. The large leaves of this marsh plant are the key aspect to its usability with frogs and toads. Photo by R. Zukal.

Cabomba caroliniana. This fully aquatic plant has more decorative value than anything else, but some aquatic species may find it a welcome egglaying spot. Photo by R. Zukal.

got Mother Nature staring you right in the face. Your own private forest!

After you've gone through the first two stages of calculating the basics of your vivarium and setting it all up, throw in a few of the extras just mentioned. A large rock, or indeed a few to an otherwise bland context than just about anything imaginable. These are now commercially available and among the most picturesque items you'll ever find.

Finally, anything else from your pet's natural habitat will help, i.e., if

Knowing where your anuran(s) originated will help you properly set up their captive habitat. A frog or toad from this region of the New Jersey Pine Barrens, for example, (like, perhaps, a Fowler's Toad, *Bufo woodhousei fowleri*), would need a fairly dry setup. Photo by W. P. Mara.

medium-sized to small ones, placed thoughtfully, adds a whole new visual dimension to any environment.

A sturdy branch or two, especially for the arboreal species, is also a must. Maybe the anurans you have won't hop right on it, but it certainly looks nice.

A parcel of driftwood seems to add more flavor you know your specimen is native to, say, the Pine Barrens of the eastern United States, then a few pine cones would look nice.

On the more practical side of this topic, remember that whatever you use is going to have to be cleaned or disposed of (unless of course, like the plants, it's living).

If, for whatever reason, you *must* keep frogs or toads *en masse*, only do it on a temporary basis, i.e., a day or so at the most. Photo by Isabelle Francais, courtesy of Tom Crutchfield.

When you must resort to overcrowding, be sure the anurans have plenty of moisture. With as many as are shown in this tank (Green Treefrogs, *Hyla cinerea*), a pump-spray bottle may not be enough; you may have to use a hose like this gentleman is doing. Photo by Isabelle Francais, courtesy of Tom Crutchfield.

If you take the time to carefully plant and arrange your frog or toad's tank, you may find the setup as pleasing to the eye as the animals themselves. Many frog and toad keepers get their start as junior horticulturists this way. Photo by Isabelle Francais, courtesy of Eric Anderson.

Branches will either have to be scrubbed or replaced (the latter is preferable), as will rocks and so forth.

The best overall advice I can give you for the decorative process is to simply take the time to try different things, experiment with various setups, and then make your final decisions from there. Let your own consequences are obvious—extensive germ infestation, unattractive quarters, and worst of all, sick animals.

The proper care and maintenance of these holding areas is not a difficult process, but many keepers feel it can be a bit of a "hassle" and tend to procrastinate slightly.

Shown is a very simple highly aquatic setup that virtually anyone can create—a large leaf and a little water. Shown is a group of Ornate Horned Frogs, *Ceratophrys ornata*, who are not terribly aquatic and thus will spend much of their time on the leaf. Photo by Isabelle Francais, courtesy of Joe Fauci.

personal taste guide your judgment. When you've finally reached that "magic" combination of sticks, stones, and plant life, you'll know it.

GENERAL TANK MAINTENANCE

Every now and then your pets' cage will need a good, thorough cleaning. If this is not attended to at regular intervals, the

However, if you look at it from the animal's point of view you will see that you have no real choice in the matter; they are certainly not going to do it on their own! You must learn to attune yourself to the fact that it simply must be done. Motivate yourself by thinking about how beautiful a freshly cleaned tank looks.

Since the basics of tank

Perhaps the only bad part about setting up a nicely arranged tank is having to break it back down to clean it. This however, is a must because frogs and toads are remarkably sensitive to filthy surroundings. Photo by Isabelle Francais, courtesy of Tim M. Scott.

cleaning are rather obvious (remove inmates, clean all reusable decor, i.e., rocks, gravel, water bowls, etc., dispose of and replace others, etc., etc., etc.), there is no real reason to do a step-by–step instruction here. However, some time-tested helpful hints might prove useful—

1) When scrubbing an empty tank, try a mixture of warm water, soft soap, and a little bleach. The soap will do most of the general work, but the bleach kills off the heavy germs. Wash with warm, and rinse very thoroughly in cold. This mixture can also be used for most of the reusable decor (except branches), and the gravel bedding as well. Remember, a little bleach goes a long way, and heavy rinsing is essential.

2) Try to avoid using scrub pads. Scratched glass looks awful.

3) When cleaning, place aquatic frogs in a separate container of water that is roughly the same temperature the tank water was. If you don't, the shock could be damaging to the animal.

4) If you have a mated adult pair of frogs or toads in the same tank, be careful removing things; you never know. Amphibian eggs are extremely delicate and usually hard to notice, especially if you're not expecting any.

5) Finally, most animals appreciate a little variety in their settings. After you've cleaned the tank, arrange it differently than before.

To add a little visual variety to your anurans' setup, purchase a piece of scenic sheeting, available in a variety of tableaux at many pet shops. Photo courtesy of Creative Surprizes.

The best kind of anurans to own are those with voracious appetites. White's Tree Frog, *Litoria caerulea*, for example, which is what this little creature is, has a reputation for voraciousness. Be careful, though—many of the same type of frogs and toads will gladly bite your fingers. Photo by Isabelle Francais.

Feeding Your Pet

Perhaps the most important aspect to be considered in any facet of animal keeping is feeding. After all, what does it matter if your frog or toad has an attractive tank, a clean pond, and a few friends, if it is not fed properly?

Therefore we must endeavor to teach ourselves every detail of correct amphibian feeding. By the end of this chapter you will have hopefully done just that.

CRICKETS

As most people probably know, frogs and toads are among a specially categorized group of living creatures known as *carnivores*. In short, this simply means they consume living flesh. Although crickets are not what you or I would exactly term as "meat," to amphibians, they are. In fact, a very large part of the diet of the anuran order consists of insects (although some in the tadpole stage may nibble on certain plants and algae every now and then). Thus, crickets, possibly the most commercially available item, make up an enormous percentage of their domestic foods.

One reason why crickets are so often utilized is probably because they're so easy to acquire. There's a very good chance almost every pet store in the world that sells frogs and toads also stocks crickets.

Another reason has to do

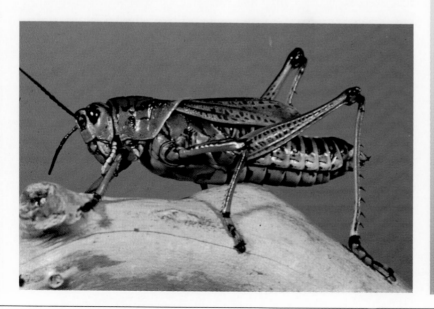

Grasshoppers make an excellent meal for frogs and toads, their only drawback being that some keepers may have trouble obtaining them on a regular basis. Photo by Paul Freed.

Crickets are, by far, the food item most often offered to captive frogs and toads. They form a complete nutritional picture and can be obtained from a number of sources, the most logical being your local pet shop. Photo by W. P. Mara.

with their high vitamin content. Crickets make such a healthy meal for frogs and toads, it would be almost insane not to utilize them.

Thirdly, crickets can be

these easy steps to get things moving:
1) To start with, you'll need about a 20-gallon tank (ten is too little, and with more than 20 you might as well breed sheep),

maintained for a reasonably long period of time, thus giving the pet owner the convenience of simply picking out those needed, which saves a lot of trips back and forth to the store.

One route many of the more experienced keepers like to take is the breeding of their own personal cricket colony. There is certainly a lot of logic to this. If you feel confident enough to give it a whirl (and doubtless you will someday even if you don't right now), then follow

and a tight, fine-mesh top.
2) Bed the tank with a layer of sawdust.
3) Add in:
 a) about 50 to 100 adult crickets.
 b) a place for them to hide (some torn up newspapers or egg cartons)
 c) a dish with some water-soaked cotton or a sponge.
 d) a shallow bowl with some grain-type fibrous meal (corn flakes or oatmeal are both superb).
 e) perhaps a small piece of

The bite of most frogs and toads doesn't really hurt all that much, but some large specimens can break the skin. This little Budgett's Frog, *Lepidobatrachus laevis*, is fairly harmless at its present size, but when it reaches its maximum length, however—around 4.5 in/11.4 cm—it may draw a little blood. Photo by Isabelle Francais.

fruit or vegetable.

f) and a small bowl filled with lightly moistened vermiculite for the mothers to lay their eggs in.

4) Keep the temperature at a minimum of 75°F/ 24°C, and the eggs will hatch in about three weeks. When it gets close to that time, you should remove these "egg bowls" (replacing them with fresh ones simultaneously) and put

own. Rotating your breeding stock by way of replacing old adults with the new ones is a practice that should be exercised regularly. This ensures healthy continuation of the line and supplies your pets with a constant, dependable stream of food.

MEALWORMS

Another popular food item that's even easier to home-breed than crickets

A keeper should feel proud when he or she owns a frog or toad that has become so comfortable in captivity that it will do this— eat from forceps (or, even better, the keeper's fingers). Specimen shown is a small White's Tree Frog, *Litoria caerulea*. Photo by Isabelle Francais.

them in a separate container. Very often the adults will mistake the newborn young (which are extremely small—no more than an eighth of an inch in length!) for food particles and gulp them right down.

About 12 weeks after the hatchlings emerge they will achieve adult size and be ready to breed on their

are mealworms. These are the small, tubular, yellow-brownish crawly creatures you occasionally see infesting boxes of old oatmeal or cereal.

What exactly are mealworms? They are the larvae of the Flour Beetle, *Tenebrio molitor*. Although generally small, some can attain a length of well over an inch. These larger ones

can be downright scary looking and even deliver a mildly painful bite. When they're this size, the only sensible way to handle them is by using tweezers.

As most experienced hobbyists will tell you, mealworms, regardless of their price and easy breedability, will never be as well-regarded as crickets. Why? Simply because they lack so many of the essential nutrients your pets need. Sure, you can give mealworms as part of the amphibian's diet, but not

Upper photo: Mealworms and mealworm beetles make a good meal for frogs and toads, but they are not nutritionally complete unless you (lower photo) do something to them called "gut-loading," which involves feeding them multivitamins and minerals, thus making them more substantial for the anurans. Photos by Michael Gilroy (top) and Isabelle Francais (bottom).

Many of the poison frogs, family Dendrobatidae, feed on wingless fruitflies, which may be difficult for some keepers to supply. If this is your predicament, contact a biological supply house and obtain the raw materials needed to start up your own wingless fruitfly culture. Shown is a Green and Black Poison Frog, *Dendrobates auratus*. Photo by Isabelle Francais.

as the *whole* diet. This would deny them certain subtle requirements and cause them to eventually whither away to nothing. Give mealworms as a treat, but nothing more.

If you wish to try breeding mealworms, the process is, as I said before, a bit easier than breeding crickets. With mealworms you simply—

1) Purchase a small quantity (about 50) of

Maintain the surrounding temperature at about 77°F/25°C to 80°F/26°C, and in a few weeks the mothers will begin laying their eggs. Then, about 4 months later, you will have full-sized mealworms ready for serving. Of course, for the smaller frogs and toads you will want to dig through the bran matter and fish out the younger worms before they get

budding mealworms and let them transform into beetles.

2) Place these in a secure and well-ventilated container bedded with some high-fiber grain-type material (like crushed oats for ex-ample).

3) For moisture, add in some small pieces of fresh vegetable matter.

this big. That's what's so wonderful about breeding your own—the freedom of choice. One note of caution concerning the offering of some of the larger mealworms—many times these monsters will sustain even after being swallowed, and actually chew their way through the inner linings of your anuran's body. I realize

Most of the treefrogs of the genus *Hyla* do well in captivity, but some of them are quite passive in their predatory behavior and should be given very small, very weak food items (i.e., very small crickets), and furthermore not housed with more aggressive species. Shown are a pair of Spotted Tree Frogs, *Hyla punctata*, from South America. Photo by Paul Freed.

Maintaining your own mealworm culture is not difficult. You need a large plastic container (with a few small holes drilled through the top), some type of grain as a substrate (oatmeal works well), and a few pieces of fruit. Beyond that, the "bugs" will take care of themselves. Photo by Isabelle Francais, courtesy of Mark B. Robertson.

how revolting that sounds, but it's true nevertheless. To avoid this, you can either boil them, stick them in the refrigerator for a few moments (thus slowing them down considerably), or simply whack their heads with a mallet and then wiggle their corpses (via tweezers) in front of

your pets will know what to do with.

FLIES

Another fine food for your hungry anuran friends is the fly. There are, needless to say, hundreds and hundreds of different species in existence, and none of them (at least the ones in

the hungry animal so as to simulate movement.

Finally, you should change your breeding stock every so often (about 50 to 100 each month) to assure yourself a strong, dependable flow. By adhering to this simple rule you will have more mealworms than

your immediate area) are terribly difficult to obtain.

For some of the smaller frogs and toads, the common housefly is a good item. Obviously these would be somewhat difficult to breed, but in the warmer months they can be caught by way

Some particularly aggressive frog species, like this large Ornate Horned Frog, *Ceratophrys ornata*, should be fed with forceps rather than with your fingers; the fingers may become part of the meal too! Photo by Isabelle Francais, courtesy Tim M. Scott.

Some food items, like these termites (being looked upon with great interest by two Dyeing Poison Frogs, *Dendrobates tinctorius*), can be offered on shallow plastic trays or cups. Two advantages to this is that you can easily keep track of what has been eaten and what hasn't, and you won't make a mess on the substrate. Photo by Isabelle Francais, courtesy of Eric Anderson.

your own easy-to-make flytrap.

This will consist of a large mesh tube or cubical (about one foot wide and two feet high) with a hole in the bottom leading into a short funnel (about 6 to 8 in/ 15.2 to 20.3 cm). This is set about 6 in/15.2 cm off the ground with the funnel entrance left open and a small chunk of

no time at all. These can be secured with a wet mesh net and then transferred into a jar until needed.

Another preferred item in this category is the common fruitfly. If you've ever left a small section of apple or orange lying about for too long then you've no doubt seen these tiny little creatures. They too can be caught

Pillbugs are taken readily by most frog and toad species, but they usually are not offered for sale in pet shops. However, many keepers will be able to find them right in their own backyard. Photo by Jim Bateman.

effective bait underneath. Again, rotten fruit is good, but with flies you can pretty much leave just about anything. Checking the trap daily, you should find yourself with a nice selection in

and even bred (to an extent) by placing a small container of decimated banana peels in your backyard (again, during the warmer months), with a smaller version of the above mentioned funnel

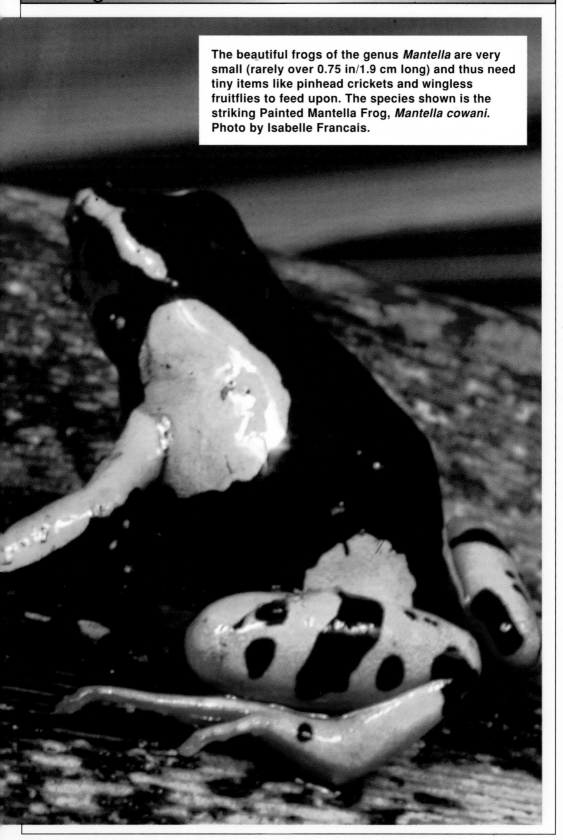

The beautiful frogs of the genus *Mantella* are very small (rarely over 0.75 in/1.9 cm long) and thus need tiny items like pinhead crickets and wingless fruitflies to feed upon. The species shown is the striking Painted Mantella Frog, *Mantella cowani*. Photo by Isabelle Francais.

extending downward from the top. In time, if this trap is left alone, the flies will feel comfortable enough to begin laying eggs and thus you will have started a small colony. If you set out a few more of these traps you'll probably end up with more fruitflies than you'll know what to do with, but better too many than not enough. When you're ready to collect them, use the same method outlined for the houseflies, but exercise a bit more caution since fruitflies are a little more nervous and may decide to leave their new homes in search of one a little less threatening.

One aspect of frog and toad keeping that hobbyists should remember is that many species prefer to eat in the dark (and, obviously, in private) and thus are best fed after "light out." Photo of a Spotted Tree Frog, *Hyla punctata*, by Paul Freed.

EARTHWORMS

Now here's a creature many of us are well-acquainted with—the earthworm. Anyone who's spent time fishing knows all about these.

Nice part is, most frogs and toads relish earthworms, and they're highly nutritious too. In fact, if your were to limit your pets' diet to nothing but earthworms, crickets, and perhaps the occasional vitamin supplement, they would probably never need anything else for the rest of their lives.

Another fine point about earthworms is that you can obtain them by the dozen right in your

Some frog species, like this handsome yet bizarre-looking Asian Horned Frog, *Megophrys nasuta*, have a reputation for being "hardy," and "voracious," meaning they'll eat just about anything. These are, obviously, ideal terrarium inmates. Get to know which species are which; it may be crucial to the decision concerning your choice of pet. Photo by Paul Freed.

own backyard (if, of course, you have a backyard or similar). Choose a small parcel of land about 3 to 5 ft/91.4 to 152.4 cm square, cover it with about a two-inch layer of leaves, small wood chips, or mulch, then cover that with a large towel (old beach towels are good), and, once a day, travel out there and wet it down with fine mist from a garden hose with the nozzle attachment. After a few days the worms will begin to surface, and then there they'll be for the choosing. When that local supply runs out (which it will eventually), simply shift the setup into a another area. By the time you've covered all the ground the first patch will be ready again.

If you don't have a backyard (or similar), then what can you do? Most pet stores don't sell worms for any reason (since they already stock crickets and mealworms), but bait stores do. If you decide to visit one be sure you get the right size for your pets—a foot-long night crawler may be all fine and well for a Colorado River Toad, *Bufo alvarius*, but it certainly isn't going to do a Spring Peeper, *Pseudacris crucifer*, much good. And if the bait store in question isn't local, be sure and stock up so you don't have to travel too frequently. You can keep the excess in a small box filled with soil and place it in your refrigerator.

Your family members may have a lot to say about this, so remember to keep it subtle and let people know beforehand. Keep the top closed tight and tuck it way in the back with a "do not touch" message scrawled across it.

OTHER ITEMS

If you wish to vary your frog's or toad's diet a

fish. These items can be offered at any time and will probably be taken with great eagerness. It is generally a good idea to give you pets something a little different every now and again, so hopefully you will now have some idea as to what those variants might be.

VITAMIN SUPPLEMENTS

Although this book has

When culturing termites, use pieces of loose tree bark. Not only will the termites thrive, but the bark pieces can be placed right into the anurans' enclosure during feeding time. Photo by Isabelle Francais, courtesy of Eric Anderson.

little, even beyond the realm of what has been outlined here, a few other items you might consider trying are whiteworms, grasshoppers, pinkie mice (only for the larger species but very nutritious and highly recommended), caterpillars, spiders, locusts, and very small

been geared mainly toward the beginner, the author feels that no one, from beginner to pro, should be exempt from occasionally providing their pet with some form of vitamin supplementation. After all, your particular frog or toad may very well be in need of this someday,

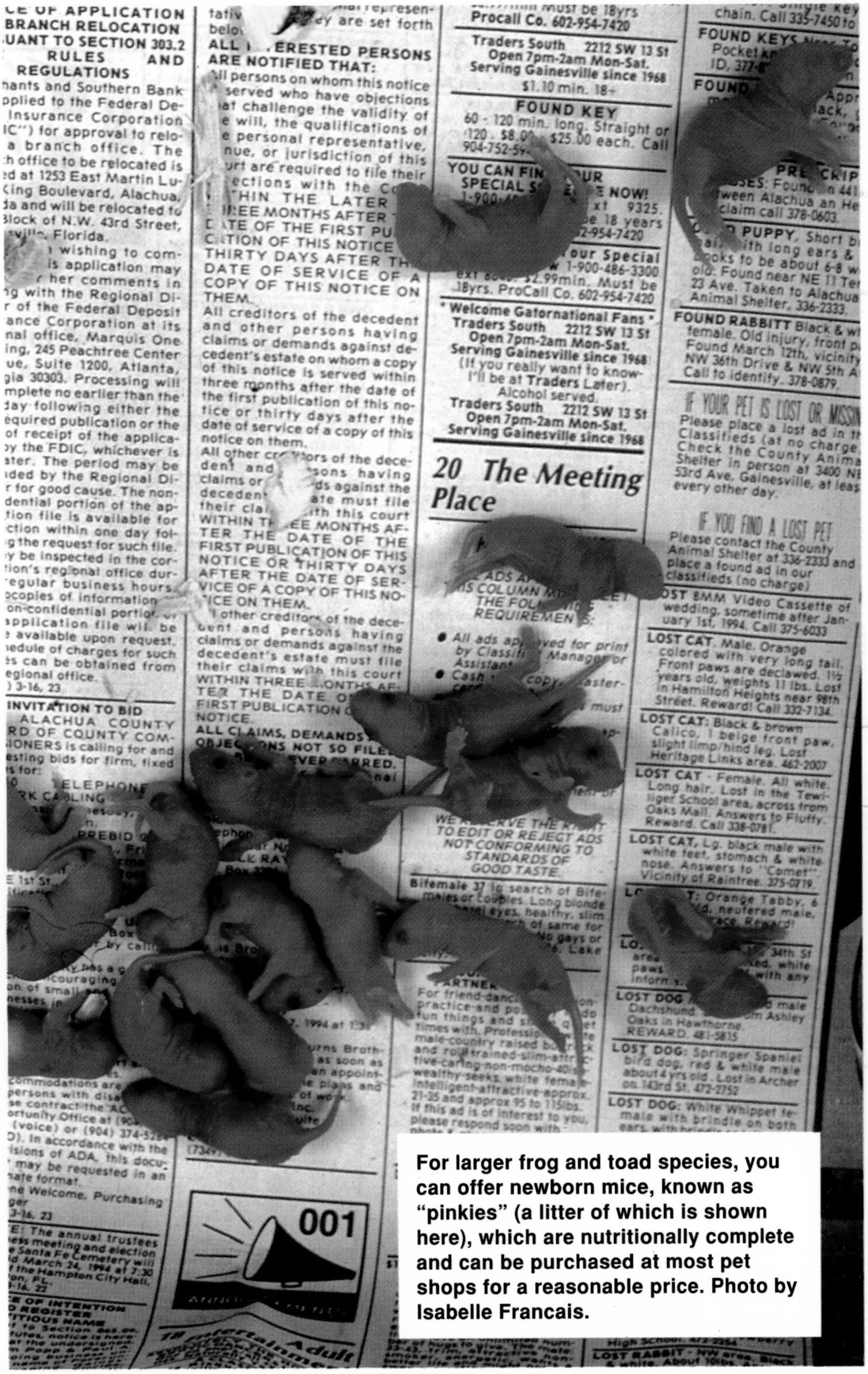

For larger frog and toad species, you can offer newborn mice, known as "pinkies" (a litter of which is shown here), which are nutritionally complete and can be purchased at most pet shops for a reasonable price. Photo by Isabelle Francais.

The African Bullfrog, *Pyxicephalus adspersus*, is a good example of an anuran species that will readily take small mice. Above, **a young specimen is being offered a "fuzzy" (a mouse that has just begun to grow hair).** Below, **a large adult finishes one off. Both photos by Isabelle Francais.**

so what kind of excuse could justify not giving it any?

The most reasonable approach to this matter is not to sit and list each vitamin they may or may not need, but to simply suggest that they receive a general multivitamin additive to their already existing meals. These can be delivered in two forms: liquid and powder. Since

we will be using them in context with frogs and toads, the powders are the easier to work with.

The technique is simple—if you have an aquatic herp, simply drop a tiny chip of vitamin pill into the water during feeding time, maybe once a month. Since most underwater anurans will jump at just about any food they see, chances

section since this may wash the vitamin film right off. Again, doing this about once a month is fine.

THE FEEDING SCHEDULE

In some ways, snake owners are very lucky— their pets only have to be fed once a week (and sometimes even less than that!). As a frog and toad keeper, you do not have

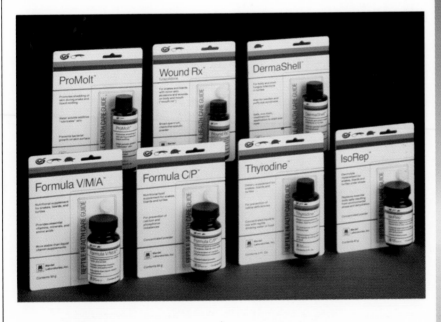

Many pet shops offer a variety of products designed to help you deal with certain at-home husbandry problems such as bad sheds, small wounds, and so on. Photo courtesy Mardel Laboratories.

are they'll take it without hesitation.

If you do not have an aquatic frog or toad, then crush the pill into fine powder, place a standard food item in a separate container, dust it heavily until it carries an adherent layer, then offer it to your pets as usual. Be careful not to drop it into the pond

such liberties at your disposal. Your pets need to be fed every other day or every third day.

This does not mean they have to be stuffed. In fact, a pondhopper left slightly hungry is better than one that can't move. Many keepers think the ideal theory is "as long as it keeps eating, feed it." This is wrong. Give them

Ideally, you can enrich any anuran food item with multivitamin liquids and/or powders, as is being done to these termites. This is not to say you should offer such supplementation at every meal; once a week is adequate. Photo by Isabelle Francais, courtesy of Eric Anderson.

Many anuran larvae, and a few adults, feed readily on various commercial fish foods. Here, an adult albino African Clawed Frog, *Xenopus laevis*, is being offered a cupful of pellet food. Photo by Isabelle Francais, courtesy Mark B. Robertson.

enough, and perhaps a little more, but that's it. Through trial and error you will learn how much this is.

Try to get them on a regular time-of-day schedule as well. If you find the most convenient time for you to feed your amphibs is in the evening hours, then feed them only in the evening hours (except of course in case of an emergency). This is, of course, not always similar to how they would find their food in the wild, but then they aren't in the wild.

Tadpole of the European Midwife Toad, *Alytes obstetricans*. Photo by M. P. and C. Piednoir.

An Introduction to Frog and Toad Breeding

Although most of the topics we've covered thus far are basic, the successful practice of breeding any captive animals will always be somewhat tricky. What I mean by this is that it requires much patience, attention to detail, and knowledge on the subject.

For example, in regards to actual reproduction, frogs and toads do not fall into one form, but eleven. These are classified as follows—

1) Egglaying Bubble-nesters
2) Egglaying Leaf-nesters
3) Egglaying Pit-nesters
4) Egglaying, with males caring for egg string
5) Egglaying, pouch-care (dorsal)
6) Egglaying, externally fertilized
7) Throat-brooders
8) Stomach-brooders
9) Poison Frogs, Type I
10) Poison Frogs, Type II
11) Live-bearing, internal fertilization

(Zimmerman, *Reptiles and Amphibians, Care-Behavior-Reproduction*, TFH Publications, H-1078)

SEX DETERMINATION

I think I can say without fear of opposition that it would be somewhat difficult to breed two frogs and/or toads together without being assured of their compatibility, i.e.,

Albino herptiles of any kind are treasured by modern herpeto-culturists, mainly because they are stunning in appear-ance. This albino Ornate Horned Frog, *Ceratophrys ornata*, for example, is a beautiful animal. Photo by W. P. Mara.

one is male and the other is female. Again, as with breeding, determining sex with anurans is just a bit more difficult than with other herps. Basically it depends on the species, but that of course means you, the breeder, must be somewhat knowledgeable of his or her own specimens.

Below is a list of outstanding traits that certain frogs and toads possess when the breeding season begins. If you wish to take the time to sort through it, perhaps you can determine the sexes of your animals. Latin classifications are generally listed, but some of the common names are included as well. If the

species you have is not included either here or in the species chapter of this book, then consult a reliable guide for further information.

—Pelobatidae (Spadefoot Toads): With the male of this species, there are a series of glands in their upper arms which will swell during the appropriate time.

—There is sometimes a notable difference in throat coloration with male Ranidae (true frogs), Microhylidae (narrow-mouthed toads), *Hyperolius* (some treefrogs), and Hylidae (general treefrogs).

—Female cloacal regions (rear vents) will swell in members of

Anurans that create foam nests, or bubble nests as they are sometimes known, usually have a large number of eggs—up to 1000 (although more around 200 to 500). Photo by John Coborn.

Pipidae (some aquatic frogs).

—Females generally larger in Bufonidae (true toads), Ranidae, Hylidae, Rhacophoridae, and Leptodactylidae (bullfrogs).

—A horizontal throat fold in some male *Phyllobates* (*femoralis*), *Bufo* (*maculatus*), Hylidae, Ranidae, Hyperolius, Dendrobatidae (poison frogs) *Bufo*, Rhacophoridae,

"Amplexus" is the word for the locking together of male and female anurans during mating. Notice how the male's grasp can vary— Above, (Amazon Basin Treefrog, *Hyla boans*), the female is being held on the upper part of the front legs, just under the chin. Photo by Paul Freed. Below, (Cristate Toad, *Bufo cristatus*) the male holds her just above and behind the armpits. Photo by R. D. Bartlett.

Microhylidae, and Leptodactylidae.

—"Finger pads" present in some male members of *Bufo*, *Chiromantis*, *Bombina* (Firebelly Toads), *Litoria*, and *Rana*.

—A trio of distinct cloacal skin folds in female *Xenopus*.

(Zimmerman, *Reptiles and Amphibians, Care-*

keepers want to know which ones are which long before that time comes around.

DETERMINING "BREEDABILITY"

Once you have gone through the process of figuring males from females, the next question to ask is "are these two

A simple way of separating tadpoles that you suspect (or know) are cannibalistic is to place them in large plastic cups. Photo by Isabelle Francais, courtesy of Eric Anderson.

Behavior-Reproduction, TFH Publications, H-1078)

Most assuredly this small table does not list everything, but covers many anurans often seen in captivity. Of course, males can almost always be distinguished because of their mating calls (which many people have heard on wet spring nights). However, most

amphibians in breeding condition?" Put simply, this asks, have they been provided with the required climatic conditions that trigger the breeding hormones, and are they in good health?

Firstly, every species of frog and toad must go through some sort of "rest cycle" whereby they are convinced the seasons are

Tadpoles housed in large cups can also be fed there, but you must remember that the water will get filthy more quickly and thus have to be changed more often. With only a few tadpoles, this may not be a big deal, but when you are breeding *en masse*, you will have a real measure of tedium to look forward to. Photo by Isabelle Francais, courtesy of Eric Anderson.

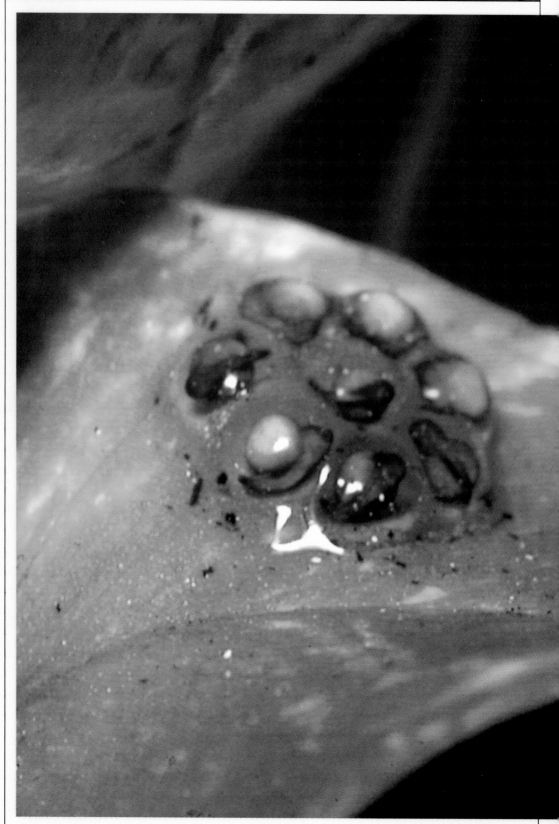

One of the most fascinating aspects of breeding behavior in many poison frogs, family Dendrobatidae, is the guarding of egg clutches. Such a trait is quite advanced in the lower vertebrate world and suggests a degree of mental development not usually attributed to amphibians. Species shown is a male Ecuadorean Poison Frog, *Epipedobates bilinguis*. Photo by Isabelle Francais, courtesy of Eric Anderson.

If you look closely, you will be able to see the fine layer of protective skin this Ornate Horned Frog, *Ceratophrys ornata*, is trying to remove after its term of estivation. Photo by Paul Freed.

changing. For example, if you have a Pickerel Frog, *Rana palustris*, and you do not hibernate it, then it will not know spring from fall and breeding will not commence.

Even in the case of captive-bred animals, it is always best to replicate the natural situation if you wish to assure smooth proceedings. Take the time to learn about your particular pet's natural history. What is its environment like in the winter? Can you faithfully import these details into your own home? You should be able to.

ARTIFICIAL HIBERNATION

As I said before, many frogs and toads will have to be artificially hibernated before breeding can begin. It is a natural process in the wild, and must thus become the same indoors as well. Of course, you will have to learn whether or not your particular pets fall into the "hibernating" (or "temperate zone") category, but if they do, there is a fairly simple procedure you can follow to get sufficient results:

1) About two weeks before you wish hibernation to begin, gradually start shortening photoperiod by about fifteen minutes per day, and lowering heat by about three degrees per day.

2) At the end of this time, put your breeders in separate plastic shoeboxes (males and females can be conglomerated, but if you are unaware of the sexes then house them individually. This should not be too much of a problem since they don't require much space anyway), bedding the boxes with something like moist vermiculite, sphagnum moss, or potting soil. And don't forget to drill a few small holes in the lid for air circulation. They don't need much, but they do need some.

3) Place the containers in a refrigerator with the temperature set between 40 and 47°F/4 and 9°C (43 to 45°F/6 to 7°C being the safest

If you are fortunate enough to have male frogs or toads that will call in your presence, you will no doubt notice that these calls often are very pleasing to the ear. Shown is a male Bird-voiced Treefrog, *Hyla avivoca*, in mid-call. Photo by R. D. Bartlett.

If anurans lay so many eggs, how come there aren't that many anurans? Because many egg masses are laid in or near streams, lakes, ponds, and so on (like these of a *Rana dalmatina*), and are thus vulnerable to predators, bad weather, mankind, etc. It is thought that only about 5 % of all anuran eggs hatch, transform, and grow to full adulthood. Photo by M. P. and C. Piednoir.

and most preferable). If you think the people you live with will find the idea of opening the door and seeing amphibians hibernating inside a bit revolting (although why would they?), you can place the containers in a

allowed to execute the above procedure (and this would be a true shame since frogs and toads are one of the few herps you can dependably hibernate in a normal refrigerator), then your only other option is to simply wait for the winter cold to

cardboard box with a few holes punched in it. This puts the animals in question well out of sight, and once they've been tucked safely away in the back and on the bottom, nobody will even remember they're there after awhile.

If you find yourself in the unenviable position of absolutely not being

arrive and do it for you (unless of course you live in a tropical or neo-tropical region, in which case it's the fridge route or no breeding at all).

Of course, this process can be somewhat controlled as well, at least within the confines of your home. What you need to do is find a spot in your house where the temperature can be

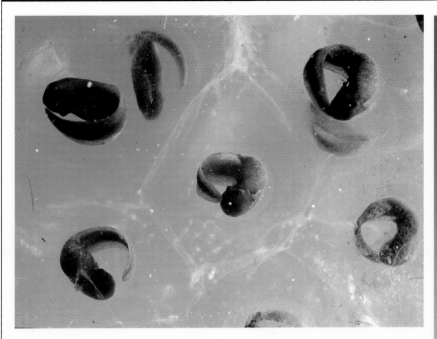

allowed to drop to the aforementioned level. Once you have located this place (it will usually be the basement or attic), you must next make sure you have access to an electrical outlet so you can run a thermostat-controlled heater in case the temperature dips too low. Since the weather fluctuates so much, you cannot afford to wholly rely on it; it is simply too risky. If you do not have a heater already then I highly suggest the small,

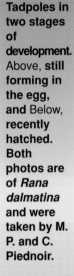

Tadpoles in two stages of development. Above, **still forming in the egg,** and Below, **recently hatched. Both photos are of *Rana dalmatina* and were taken by M. P. and C. Piednoir.**

Only male anurans have vocal sacs, used primarily to call for mates during the breeding season. These sacs can be paired or single, the latter of which can be seen on this Mountain Treefrog, *Hyla eximia*. Photo by K. H. Switak.

cube-shaped, ceramic models. They're both inexpensive and efficient, not to mention cheap to run, and chances are they have some sort of thermostat already built in. If they don't, or if you already have a heater and that one doesn't have a thermostat either, you can purchase a clever little device that plugs into the wall, houses the heater's plug behind it's own, and then, when the surrounding temperature reaches a certain point (predetermined by you via a small dial), it will allow current to pass and the heater will kick on. This is

a marvelous way to control seemingly uncontrollable climates, and I strongly recommend you look into purchasing one if the need arises.

DURING HIBERNATION

Now that you have your frogs and toads in their containers and the thermometer is reading 46°F/8°C, what's next?

Not much actually. Nature will take over, and your participation will become quite minimal. There will be no food or water requirements, nor will there be any cleaning duties to perform.

However, there are

always a few standard "maintenance measures" you will need to get into the habit of attending to. One is, if you have you were lucky enough to put your pets in a refrigerator, make sure the door is opened for about one minute everyday to allow fresh air replacement. If you have them in your standard kitchen fridge then this really doesn't need to be done since normal usage will suffice.

If you have them in a different unit, however, like the small cube types, then this practice must be carried out faithfully. (Incidentally, if you are thinking about eventually getting seriously involved in the breeding side of this hobby, then it might not be a bad idea to track down one of these same small fridges just for this purpose. They can be acquired through flea markets, garage sales, hotel or motel going out of business sales, or through a private college student who just graduated and is selling the contents of his or her dorm room. The convenience is unparalleled—you can theoretically hibernate

Many frogs and toads can be distin-guished simply by their calls, and some species are so similar in other character-istics that only their calls delineate them. Photo of a Little Grass Frog, *Pseudacris ocularis*, by R. D. Bartlett.

your breeders whenever you wish. This gives light to some intriguing possibilities.)

Another thing you will want to do, about every four or five days or so, is open the amphibs' container and lightly mist the contents. This maintains a reasonable moisture level, which is what they would experience if they were hibernating in the wild.

Other than those two duties, there really isn't much for the hobbyist to do while their pets are at rest. If the thought of this bothers you, then perhaps you can try something I used to do: buy a few "non-breeder" anurans to keep you company all year long. Many "herpers" (as herpetocultural hobbyists are sometimes called) do this in order to keep their interests satisfied during the slower, colder months. If you think this is something you'll do, then be sure obtain species that are either captive-bred, or naturally non-hibernating. To simply deny them their enforced rest for the sake of your own pleasure is somewhat cruel (not to mention it cuts down their lifespan slightly), but if you choose a pet that does not need it in the first place then there is no cause for concern.

Frogs and toads should generally be hibernated for a period of six to ten weeks, depending again on their locality. Again, consult reliable sources when garnering this information.

AFTER HIBERNATION

When the time comes to remove your pets from their rest period, you

Most treefrogs, *Hyla* sp., make wonderful captives, but strangely, many species seem unwilling to breed. Photo of two European Treefrogs, *Hyla arborea*, by Michael Gilroy.

If you wish to try your hand at captive-breeding any frogs or toads, do yourself a favor and only obtain species that have a reputation for being easily "breedable." White's Tree Frog, *Litoria caerulea*, is a good example of such a species. Photo by Isabelle Francais.

must take special care to ease them out of it slowly, as opposed to simply carrying the containers from the cold to the heat.

Warm them gradually, raising their surrounding temperature about five to ten degrees every two hours. If they are in the refrigerator, this may not be possible. In that case, simply place them in a cool room (about 65 to 70°F/18 to 21°C) and let them thaw out that way. If that is not the case, then follow the aforementioned instructions to the best of your ability.

When it becomes obvious they have returned to an active state (they will move about without sluggish restriction), continue to keep them well-separated and give them about a day to readjust to the world around them. Many hibernating animals, whether it be frogs and toads or otherwise, will experience a short period of "disorientation" and behave uncharacteristically. The only way to cure this is through time, so give them some.

After that, you can begin feeding them normally again, and then, shortly afterwards, the breeding cycle can begin.

BREEDING

As I said before, the biggest problem with breeding anurans is having to know what needs to be done with

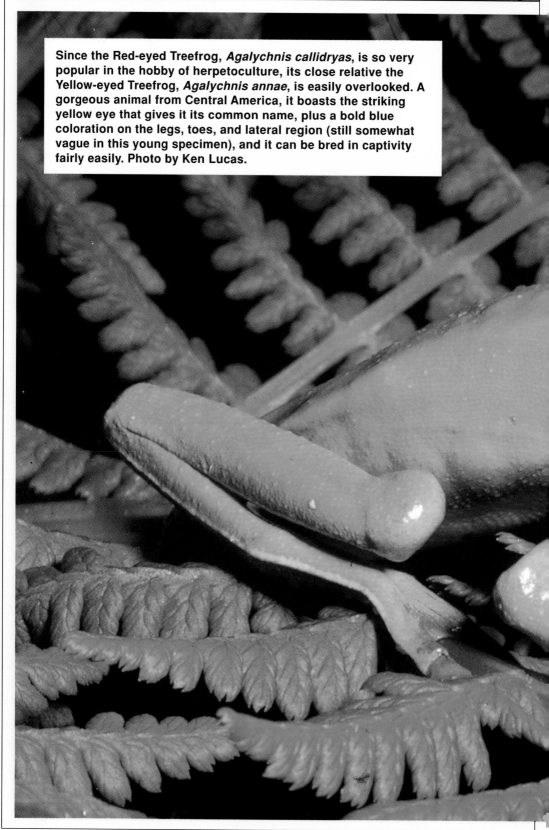

Since the Red-eyed Treefrog, *Agalychnis callidryas*, is so very popular in the hobby of herpetoculture, its close relative the Yellow-eyed Treefrog, *Agalychnis annae*, is easily overlooked. A gorgeous animal from Central America, it boasts the striking yellow eye that gives it its common name, plus a bold blue coloration on the legs, toes, and lateral region (still somewhat vague in this young specimen), and it can be bred in captivity fairly easily. Photo by Ken Lucas.

what species. If you are willing to take the time to do this, then you will probably meet with some level of success. Keep in mind that some are easier to breed than others, and many have never been bred in captivity at all. That's not to say they're impossible, just simply that no one's ever

—Set up a separate breeding tank, and place the male in first. When he begins to trill, enter the female.

—Climatic conditions are the key to breeding any frog or toad. If you're serious about what you're trying to do, then go to the trouble of learning what goes on in their

As you can tell by this picture of a newly meta-morphosed Southern Tomato Frog, *Dyscophus guineti*, baby anurans are not terribly large. They aren't very strong, either, so don't hibernate them until they've grown a few years. Photo by Paul Freed.

dedicated time to them yet.

It obviously would be pointless to outline a step-by-step instruction for breeding here since I have no idea which animals you have, but it might still be useful to include a list of "helpful hints" that have some synchronicity with all species concerned.

natural environment. Find out exactly what leads them to breed. Many species, particularly in the tropical rainforest areas, needs warm, heavy downpours to trigger procreation. Others depend heavily on photoperiods. Learn the details, then simulate them. Most of the trouble lies in actually getting the information; creating the scenario usually isn't the hard part at all.

—Do yourself a favor and use only real foliage in a breeding tank.

—After you've witnessed the copulation (and you should always make a point to do this) and you are sure the

From learning this you can pretty much understand just how delicate amphibian eggs are.

—Do not vary the surrounding conditions of the eggs whatsoever, unless they are naturally laid out of water, in which case an increase in humidity may be

Frogs and toads will need as much food and as varied a diet as possible during their formative years. This is time when the most demands are made on the keeper. Photo of a newly meta-morphosed water-holding frog, *Cyclorana* sp., by Paul Freed.

species involved do not trouble themselves with brood care, remove the pair immediately. In the wild, most eggs will never hatch due to destructive factors such as consumption by other animals, those same animals crushing them inadvertently while moving about, and so on.

required. Severe climatic fluctuation will damage, and probably destroy, most of them. Tadpoles emerge shortly after eggs are laid. When they do, it is best to find a way to separate the tadpoles. Some can be kept together, but try to avoid overcrowding.

CARING FOR THE YOUNG

Congratulations, you've done it! You've taken the time to learn what needed to be learned and now you're staring down into a tank filled with some very feisty tadpoles, swimming around like mad with no sense of direction whatsoever.

What do you do now?

Caring for the young of any animal is probably pride that grips herpetoculturists when caring for young that exist in part because of their own efforts. Naturally you want those same young to be well cared for so they can grow into healthy, active adults. Therefore, step one is to get them eating.

Unlike their parents, tadpoles are not strictly carnivorous. In the wild, they also feed on things

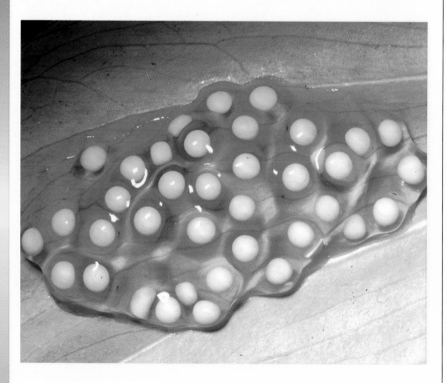

Dealing with anuran eggs can be a tricky affair; most of them are alarmingly delicate. This is one good reason you should set up a separate tank for egglaying then remove the frogs or toads afterwards. That way, the eggs needn't be touched at all. Photo of a clutch of Red-eyed Treefrog, *Agalychnis callidryas*, eggs, by Michael Gilroy.

the most rewarding, although demanding, part of the hobby. This becomes even more enjoyable when you've bred the creatures yourself. There's always that strange brand of like light plant matter and different forms of algae. In captivity, you will have to experiment to see what your young might take. Since most frog and toad larvae are omnivorous, meaning the

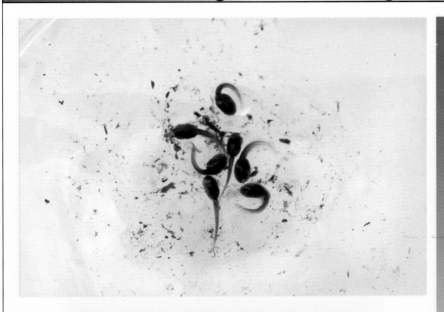

Anuran tadpoles (Above) are very small and show very little visual clues as to what they will look like after meta-morphosis. If you decide to use the individual cup method of tadpole housing, be sure to clean the cups with the help of a small piece of screening (Below) so as not to drop or otherwise injure the tads. Both photos Isabelle Francais, courtesy of Eric Anderson.

Whatever frog or toad species you decide to keep, if your specimens are adults, like this handsome African Bullfrog, *Pyxicephalus adspersus*, you should make at least some attempt to breed them. If nothing else, you will garner some experience, and it is worth remembering that just because a certain species has never been bred before doesn't mean it can't be; perhaps it's simply because it hasn't ever been tried! Photo by Isabelle Francais.

The advantage to setting up a naturalistic breeding area is so your anurans can function as closely in captivity to the way they would in the wild. These Ecuadorean Poison Frog, *Epipedobates bilinguis*, eggs, for example, have been laid on a plant leaf, and should be left there rather than removed to a different location. Photo by Isabelle Francais, courtesy of Eric Anderson.

feed on both animal and vegetable substances, at least you'll have a broad spectrum to work with. A few of the more commonly used items include water plants, untreated green leafy vegetables, dry fish food (crushed into powder), need all the nutrients they can get), and not to feed too many tadpoles together in the same tank. This will result in heavy competition for food, and may cause some specimens to damage each other. Like I said earlier, it may be

commercial baby fish food (not the liquids), mosquito larvae, certain brine shrimp, dead fruitflies, and even other amphibian eggs. Of course, this does not cover the entire list of choices at your disposal, but at least you have some suggestions to work with.

Finally, remember to vary their diet as much as possible (in these early stages they will a bit of a hassle to separate each and every one, but for many reasons it is the safest approach.

GROWTH OF THE YOUNG

Now that you have gone through the trying first stages of frog and toad reproduction, i.e., the breeding, laying of eggs, and then caring of the young, you must continue your efforts until each member of

The process of metamorphosis is immensely fascinating. Here, a European Midwife Toad, *Alytes obstetricans*, has sprouted its front and hind limbs, yet still retains its tail. This should disappear altogether within a few weeks. Once completely terrestrial, the animal will begin eating regularly within a week or two. Photo M. P. and C. Piednoir.

Once a tadpole gets close to the completion of its metamorphosis, you should provide it with either shallower water or, even better, a body of land onto which it can crawl. Shown is the transforming tadpole of a Dyeing Poison Frog, *Dendrobates tinctorius*. Photo by Isabelle Francais, courtesy of Eric Anderson.

Shown is an Ornate Horned Frog, *Ceratophrys ornata*, in two stages of development. Above, it is still a true tadpole, in the aquatic stage. Below, it has become terrestrial with its tail only partially absorbed. Both photos by Jerry R. Loll.

The captive-breeding of rare and endangered species should be encouraged at every turn, for many of these animals one day may exist only in captivity. Shown is a developing tadpole (Above) and a breeding pair (Below) of Golden Harlequin Frogs, *Atelopus zeteki*, a species which is heavily protected by environmental law. Both photos by Alex Kerstitch.

Tadpole of a Bronze Frog, *Rana clamitans clamitans*. Photo by R. D. Bartlett.

your stock has grown into full-fledged adulthood. This means adequate care on every rung of the growth ladder—a continuing healthy diet, proper surroundings, and regular sanitary maintenance.

An anuran becomes a full-grown tadpole after a relatively short time (many will do this after six to eight weeks). Shortly after this they will transform into tiny frogs or toads, then another one to four years before they reach sexual maturity. Again, as with every facet of frog and toad breeding, the exact times depends on the species, but this kind of information is not difficult to come by.

Above: Newly metamorphosed anurans, like this tiny Mexican Treefrog, *Pachymedusa dachnicolor*, may have a distinct "point" where the tail was, but this too will vanish in time. Below: Perhaps the most positive aspect of breeding frogs and toads in captivity is that the percentage of eggs that will hatch and grow into adulthood is much higher than it would be in the wild. Shown are a pair of rare Houston Toads, *Bufo houstonensis*, in amplexus, laying egg strings. Photo by Paul Freed.

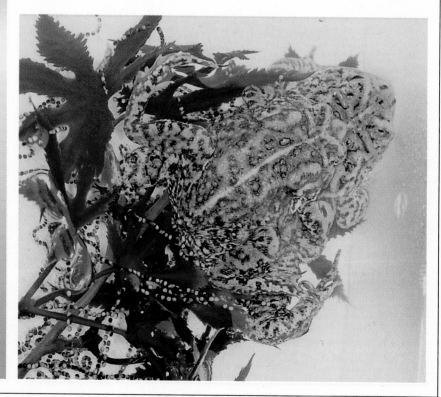

Sickness and Health

In this chapter you will learn about some of the basic illnesses your pets may fall victim to, how to treat them, and more importantly, how to avoid them in the first place.

But before we go any further, I feel there is something that needs to be said about attempts to treat sick animals at home. Quite simply, if you are not a qualified vet then you are not a qualified vet. The purpose of sharing certain treatment information with a beginner is not so he or she can fancy themselves as being one step away from opening their own office, but to provide them with the means to help some of the more mild cases without succumbing to the possibly unnecessary expense of a professional. Many times this will be exactly the case and a trained individual will not have to be consulted.

But not always. You must learn to face the fact that anytime you allow a normally wild animal into your home you run the risk of having it become so sick that it may need qualified medical attention. Along with that goes the reality that during such times your own personal skills will simply not be sufficient. Once you have accepted this, then you are in the proper frame of mind.

PREVENTIVE MEASURES

This section will not be particularly lengthy since even a person who has never housed a pet in his or her life can pretty much assume what the ramifications are.

1) **Cleanliness**—The apocalyptic factor in any captive creature's health. If you leave them in a dirty tank, they will get sick. If attending to them is too much trouble for you, then don't keep any animals. It requires time, effort, and most of all, attention to detail. Set a regular cleaning schedule and stick to it faithfully.

2) **Proper Feeding**— Beware of what you give your pets, for they may find their food more dangerous than anything else. With something like insects, you always run the risk of internal infection, that's why it's best to either breed your own or purchase them. Many fall victim to

Cleanliness is undoubtedly one of the most important details in the keeping of amphibians. It is part of something called *preventive medicine*, and should be practiced regularly by all keepers. Once of an amphibian falls ill, its chances of survival usually are quite small. Photo by Isabelle Francais, courtesy of Merilyn and Charles Abbott.

certain poisons and sprays in the outdoors, so be careful what you choose in your or someone else's backyard.

3) **Avoid Too Much Handling and Tank Movement**—Frogs and toads can sustain a variety injuries this way. Perhaps that is the one

ous, or in some obscure part of the room where it can't be reached anyway.

Excessive tank movement is no good for them either because it rattles them somewhat and makes them feel insecure. Once you have a home set up for

saddest thing about this element of herpetoculture—the fact that frogs and toads don't really like to be handled, not to mention they're somewhat difficult to grasp in the first place. Many people have attempted to pick up a pet only to have it lurch out into space and either land on something hazard-

them let them live in it in peace.

4) **Avoid Too Many Tank Mates**—And the wrong kinds too. If you have a pretty little treefrog, *Hyla* sp., and you couple it with a fine old Colorado River Toad, *Bufo alvarius*, chances are you'll only have one pet a day or two later (Colorado River Toads will eat darn near

Overcrowding a tank is not only dangerous to the inmates' health, it is cruel and inhuman. All amphibians need some degree of free space to move around in, unlike the lack of same in this appallingly overstuffed tankful of albino African Clawed Frogs, *Xenopus laevis*. Photo by Isabelle Francais, courtesy of Mark B. Robertson.

As a general rule, anurans don't care very much for being handled, but if you must hold them, for whatever reason, remember that they are jumpy. The Squirrel Treefrog, *Hyla squirella*, shown here, for example, is likely to leap away at any time if the keeper isn't careful. Photo by Isabelle Francais.

anything). Many species prey on whatever they see moving about and don't really care if that same item happens to be one of their cousins.

On the same note, some frogs and toads are actually extremely toxic to others. The Pickerel Frog, *Rana*

duces cuts, scratches, and sometimes serious wounds.

5) **Quarantining**—When you first acquire a new frog or toad, you can never be 100 % sure if it is in perfect health. Just because it checked out at the pet store and ate right in front of you does not mean it can't

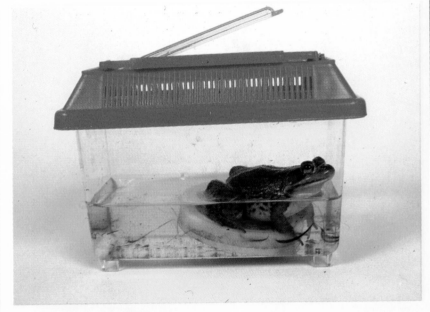

palustris, for example gives a very potent secretion from its skin, and under no circumstances should it be housed with any other species.

Finally, overcrowding should always be vigorously avoided. Cramped quarters leads to tension, stress, and ultimately fighting, which then of course pro-

spread anything to any other anurans. That's why it's good practice to quarantine every new specimen for at least a week before introducing it into an already occupied tank. The same goes for anurans you think might be sick. If you have this suspicion, isolate the animal. After all, once they've in-

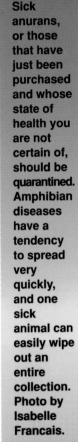

Sick anurans, or those that have just been purchased and whose state of health you are not certain of, should be quarantined. Amphibian diseases have a tendency to spread very quickly, and one sick animal can easily wipe out an entire collection. Photo by Isabelle Francais.

Every item in an anuran's tank should be washed thoroughly with soapy water and then rinsed very thoroughly or else the residues will irritate the animals' delicate and highly sensitive skin. Photo by Isabelle Francais, courtesy of Eugene L. Bessette.

fected the other ones, it's too late.

6) **Keep the Climate Steady**—Don't let light hours, humidity, temperature, or anything else that controls and formulates surrounding atmosphere deviate too much. If you want it warm, keep it warm. If the lights stay on for 12 hours everyday, then the next day it should still be 12. Allowing these things to change abruptly can seriously affect an amphibian's biological timetable, and the animal will begin to react to it. Make sure all instruments that determine these factors are unswervingly reliable and check them frequently.

If you follow the simple rules outlined here and make use of some common sense, there's no reason why a healthy anuran in your possession won't remain that way. Of course, speaking realistically, there will always be times when a frog or a toad may catch something begin to feel ill, but then that's the same with all living things. The idea with these precautionary tactics is to keep such occurrences down to a minimum; thinking you can completely eradicate the potential for disease is somewhat impractical.

As frogs and toads grow older, their tolerance for unclean surroundings increases slightly, but when they are young, it is of the utmost importance that their quarters be kept literally spotless. Photo of a young Queensland Water-holding Frog, *Cyclorana novae-hollandiae*, by R. D. Bartlett.

A tank that houses fully aquatic anurans can be kept clean easily enough—use a decent filtration system. Virtually all pet shops carry a variety of these for you to choose from. This is not to say you won't have to do *any* maintenance chores, but they will be greatly reduced. Photo of African Clawed Frogs, *Xenopus laevis*, by Isabelle Francais, courtesy of Mark B. Robertson.

Before you refill the water in your anurans' enclosure, check to see if it is close to the right temperature. Water that is too hot or too cold can easily harm a frog or a toad. Photo by Isabelle Francais, courtesy of Merilyn and Charles Abbott.

COMMON DISEASES

Red Leg

Description: Infection of upper thighs causing discoloration.

Causes: Unclean surroundings, etc. Bacteria-based.

Symptoms: Reddening of skin along upper thighs and occasionally into abdominal regions.

Suggested Treatment: Sulfamethiazine bath (15 ml

abnormal accumulation of serous bodily fluids.

Causes: Possibly bacteria, but more so improper body metabolism. This could possibly result from an inadequate diet or poor climatic maintenance.

Symptoms: Bloating, soft dermal abnormalities, particularly around the abdominal region.

Suggested Treatment: Somewhat risky in the

One way frogs and toads can get sick is by being housed with incompatible species. For example, the **Strawberry Poison Frogs,** *Dendrobates pumilio*, shown here might do fine with each other, but due to the toxic nature of their skin, they could prove deadly to frogs or toads of other genera. Learn which kinds are which before forming up your colony. Photo by Isabelle Francais.

for every 10 l water) daily for 2 weeks, or a small percentage of copper sulfate (under 5 %) and water daily for the same period. If irritation shows no sign of recession within the first week, consult a veterinarian.

Dropsy

Description: An

home. If the swelling in question is not overtly large or is located near the eyes or any other delicate externals, it is possible to puncture the spot with a sterile needle, drain the fluid, and wash the wound with a mild cleanser such as peroxide or merthiolate. Since frogs and toads will rarely sit

Green Treefrog, *Hyla cinerea*. Photo by R. D. Bartlett.

still for anyone, you may want to turn this problem over to a qualified professional.

Amoeba Infections (Internal)
Description: Parasitic amoeba invasion.
Causes: Improper or infected dietary items, unclean water, etc.
Symptoms: Hard to detect without fecal samples. Heavy liquid intake, blood in feces.
Suggested Treatment: Should only be executed by a veterinarian, since the use of certain antibiotics is required.

Worms
Description: Internal infestation of tapeworms, roundworms, flukes, etc.

Causes: Varied. Infected foods, unclean quarters. Exposure to other infected specimens.
Symptoms: Listlessness, traces of said worms and/ or worm eggs in feces, visual infestation in severe cases.
Suggested Treatment: Usually by the time you recognize this ailment it needs to be treated with antibiotics, and, in some of the more extensive cases, actual surgery may have to be performed to remove the invading parasites. When worms are suspected, a vet should be consulted immediately.

Myasis
Description: An external

The intriguing and unusual Mexican Casque-headed Treefrog, *Triprion spatulatus*, which lives in tree hollows and under heavy plant cover, coming out only during the night hours. Photo by Mella Panzella.

disease that involves attack on the host by maggots.

Causes: Tank invasion, possibly introduced by other infected parties.

Symptoms: Visible violation, especially around head.

Suggested Treatment: Removal of invading parasites via tweezers and then immediate cleansing and disinfecting of the remaining wound.

Fungal Infection

Description: Generally speaking, any notable abnormal changes in skin color.

Causes: Excessively dirty water and/or surroundings.

Symptoms: Abrupt changes in certain spots on the outer surface. In frogs and toads this is often a red inflammation based on soft white tissue.

Suggested Treatment: Coating with 8-hydroxyquinoline (one part per 5000 every other day) until condition vanishes, or consult a vet.

Abscesses

Description: A localized collection of pus in the body tissues.

Causes: Fighting with tank mates, brushes across sharp objects, etc., then the following infection.

Symptoms: Obvious lesions filled with yellow to off-white excretion. Wound should appear "infected" and "weepy."

Suggested Treatment: Cleansing of area with

This is the beautiful Sonoran Green Toad, *Bufo retiformis*. To put an aged myth to rest, no, you will not develop warts from handling toads. Photo by R. D. Bartlett.

Unlike the toads-giving-you-warts fable, you can indeed develop a number of skin problems from prolonged contact with poison frogs, of the family Dendrobatidae. Some species actually may cause death, but most, like this gorgeous Dyeing Poison Frog, *Dendrobates tinctorius*, will merely make your skin itch or burn a little. In short, frogs that belong to this family simply should not be handled. Photo by R. D. Bartlett.

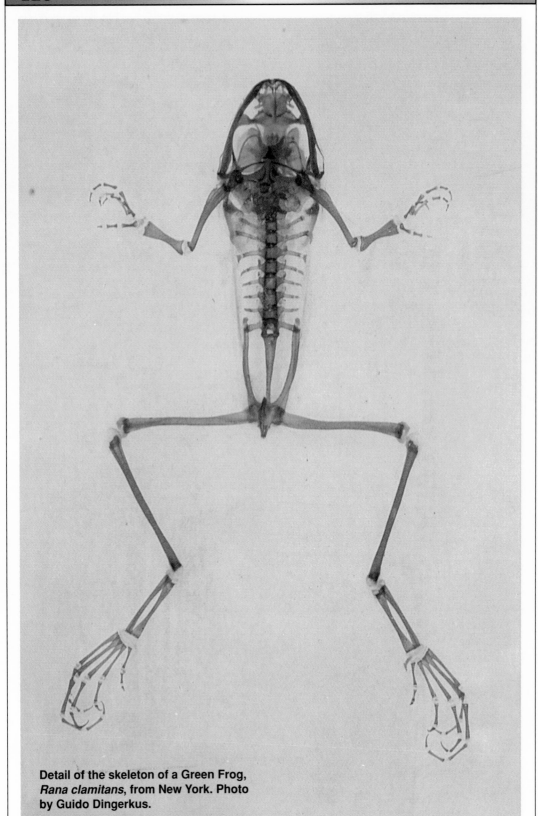

Detail of the skeleton of a Green Frog,
Rana clamitans, from New York. Photo
by Guido Dingerkus.

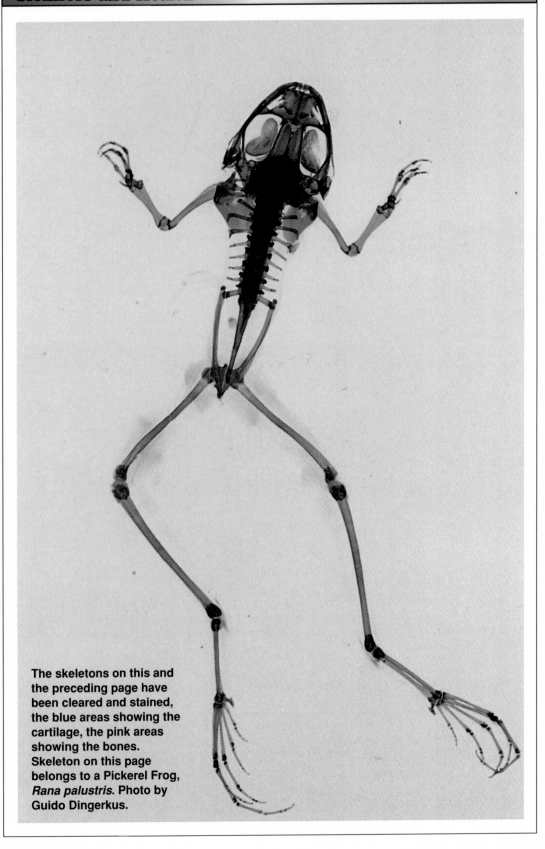

The skeletons on this and the preceding page have been cleared and stained, the blue areas showing the cartilage, the pink areas showing the bones. Skeleton on this page belongs to a Pickerel Frog, *Rana palustris*. Photo by Guido Dingerkus.

mild disinfectant (hydrogen peroxide diluted 50/50 in water), then application of "soft" antibacterial ointment. This should be done twice a day until abscess has cleared. Call a vet if it grows rather than reduces.

Rickets

Description: Lack of certain vitamin and mineral elements causing metabolic imbalances.

Causes: Inadequate diet, lack of supplementation.

least once a week until conditions recede. Then, regular supplementation once every 2 weeks.

Repeated Vomiting

Description: Patient will return everything they swallow, either immediately or sometime before complete digestion.

Causes: Varied. Usually internal parasites or viruses, but can be many things.

Symptoms: Vomiting after each meal.

Southern Cricket Frog, *Acris gryllus*. Photo by R. D. Bartlett.

Symptoms: Poor growth development. Occasional paralysis.

Suggested Treatment: Immediate dietary supplementation, most accessibly in the form of multivitamin powders lightly sprinkled on food items at

Suggested Treatment: Since repeated vomiting can be caused by some many different problems, it is best to consult a veterinarian first. Sometimes the ailment can be treated at home other times it can be more extensive.

Protruding Intestines

Description: Small lengths of intestine protruding from cloacal region.

Causes: Over-crowding, poorly maintained tanks, other general

conditions caused by poor husbandry.

Symptoms: Obvious protrusions from the aforementioned location.

Suggested Treatment: Gentle replacement of organ by way of sterilized cotton manipulated by the fingers, then immediate

Mites

Description: External invasion by mites.

Causes: Usually from other infected animals that have been introduced to the collection.

Symptoms: Lack of appetite, flaking of skin, and visible infestation of skin tissue.

Suggested Treatment: Extensive bathing in lukewarm water as an attempt to "drown" parasites until problem has cleared. Afterward, swabbing of damaged areas with

Eastern Spadefoot Toad, *Scaphiopus holbrooki*. Photo by R. D. Bartlett.

attention to patient's surrounding conditions. If the problem seems minute, it can be handled by the keeper. If the protruded area seems slightly infected, then a vet should be consulted immediately.

peroxide solution (25 % to water). If this fails, contact veterinarian.

Scab Disease

Description: Small, dark-colored growths on skin.

Causes: Usually viral.

Symptoms: Obvious

growths. These should be checked for periodically. Harder to detect on toads.

Suggested Treatment: You usually will have to contact a veterinarian. Area in question should be removed with sterile scalpel and then treated first with disinfectant and finally with protective ointment covering.

Broken Bones

Description: Bone fractures

Causes: Fights with tankmates, improper handling, etc.

Symptoms: Limping, obvious malformations at location of fracture.

Suggested Treatment: Only a qualified vet should handle something like an anuran fracture if any cure is to be achieved.

Poisoning

Description: An affliction that can attack both internally as well as externally.

Causes: Usually from incompatible cagemates (poisonous secretions from the skin, as in the case of the Pickerel Frog, *Rana palustris*, or many of the poison frogs, family Dendrobatidae).

Symptoms: Paralysis, sudden lack of appetite.

Suggested Treatment: Separate patient and bath in clean water. Sometimes brushing the skin with tomato soup or baking soda and water lessens the effect.

Skinniness

Description: Gradual lessening of specimen's overall weight. Sometimes the process can be very rapid.

Malayan Spadefoot Toad, *Lepto-brachium hasselti*. Photo by Mella Panzella.

Southern Toad, *Bufo terrestris*. Photo by R. T. Zappalorti.

Causes: Varied. Many things can cause a captive animal to lose its appetite.

Symptoms: Sudden refusal of food, although for no obvious reason.

Suggested Treatment: First, try to diagnose an illness. If that fails, attempt to force-feed subject by way of opening mouth and place in a small piece of an already preferred food item. If this proves too difficult, consult a professional. An anuran's condition can deteriorate very quickly, so prompt action is crucial.

When you consider the fact that this list only touches on the surface of possible diseases your frog or toad might encounter, it becomes obvious that captive herps have a lot to watch out for. But, as I said earlier, if you take the time to prevent illness, then matters should never get that much out of hand. Occasionally it may happen, but at least when it does you'll be prepared.

Finally, if you do fall into the unfortunate position of having one of your frogs or toads pass away, be sure to keep them frozen (in airtight bags) until a proper autopsy can be performed. That way, at least you'll know what happened. Again, this may sound a bit like going out of your way, but better to kill a problem when it has only taken one life then after it has claimed them all. Most amphibian diseases are highly contagious; stop them before they do any real damage.

A Few Interesting Species

In this chapter you will get the chance to take a fairly close look at some of the more interesting anuran species. Many are readily available in pet stores while others remain a bit more obscure to the hobbyist.

Ornate Horned Frog
Ceratophrys ornata
Description: A husky but small (usually under 7 inches) creature, attractively colored with handsome greens and dark brown to black markings, often tear–or slug-shaped, and occasionally streaks of orange or red. Belly usually yellowish white.
Geographical Range:

Argentina and parts of South America.
Natural Habitat: Moist, tropical regions.
Temperament: Unpredictable. They are eager feeders and will gladly go after whatever happens in front of them, including your fingers. They generally don't like being handled, either.
Diet: Variable. Insects, mice, other smaller vertebrates.
Response To Captivity: Does very well in captivity.
Breedability: Moderately easy, but not really recommended for beginners.
Keeping Requirements: Requires a respectable

This handsome and beautifully marked Ornate Horned Frog, *Ceratophrys ornata*, was given by the author as a present to Mr. Ray Hunziker, his good friend and also the editor of *Tropical Fish Magazine*. Virtually all the frogs of this genus make superb pets. Photo by W. P. Mara.

Note the defensive posture of this hybrid horned frog, *Ceratophrys ornata x cranwelli*. Be wary of any large, angry *Ceratophrys*, for their bites will hurt. Photo by Jim Merli.

amount of humidity and a varied, not to mention frequent, diet.

Miscellaneous Facts: In the last two decades, this animal has become one of the most popular anuran pets. Its breathtaking albeit somewhat bizarre appearance coupled with the fact that it adapts so well to captivity makes it a blue-ribbon choice among both amateur and advanced herpetologists.

Barking Treefrog
  Hyla gratiosa
  Description: Brilliant light green, yellow, or brown base color, with random dark spotting. Only about 2.5 in/6.3 cm long, and fairly plump. Skin rough.
  Geographical Range:

Southeastern U.S. coast from Virginia southward. Colonies have been imported into extreme southern New Jersey, but these are now thought to be extinct.

Natural Habitat: Among the trees during the warmer months.

Temperament: Calm, even in human presence.

Diet: Varied insects; nothing too particular.

Response To Captivity: Does extremely well.

Breedability: Fairly easy.

Keeping Requirements: This species requires an arboreal tank with a fair amount of humidity.

Miscellaneous Facts: The Barking Treefrog has become more and more difficult to acquire over

The Barking Treefrog, *Hyla gratiosa*, is a very reliable captive. Specimens will take vitamin-dusted crickets with great eagerness, and the low, guttural call that gives them their common name is very pretty. Photo by Isabelle Francais.

the last few years, possibly because it is not what one would call a "high-priced" animal and so many dealers don't bother supplying them. It is well-tempered, hardy, and makes a superb pet.

Budgett's Frog
Lepidobatrachus laevis
Description: A small, plump creature that at first glance probably looks more like a stone than a frog. It is a mocha-tan color and its eyes are located on the top of its smooth, half-moon head.
Geographical Range: Upper Argentina, Paraguay, and southeastern Bolivia.
Natural Habitat: Subtropical wetlands—ponds, lakes, etc. Humid regions.
Temperament:

Reasonably calm, but alert.
Diet: Insects, small fish.
Response To Captivity: Good.
Breedability: Moderately easy, but not recommended for beginners.
Keeping Requirements: Needs humidity and moisture. Also requires a deep, soft substrate.
Miscellaneous Facts: This stumpy little frog is quite a character. When approached, it will rear itself back in a defensive posture then bury itself in the ground until covered completely.

Pickerel Frog
Rana palustris
Description: Beautiful dark brown spots on a light tan base. Markings

Budgett's Frog, *Lepidobatrachus laevis*, does well in captivity, but is not recommended for beginners due to its unpredictable temperament. If given the chance, most specimens will not hesitate to bite. Photo by Isabelle Francais.

are often distinctly squarish. A very attractive animal.

Geographical Range: Almost all of the eastern half of the United States, except for the extreme southern parts and most of Illinois.

Natural Habitat: Damp, boggy areas, streams, wetlands, ponds, etc.

Temperament: Very alert and jumpy. Doesn't care for handling very much.

Diet: Basic anuran fare—insects, worms, etc.

Response To Captivity: Does well, but, due to the fact that it can poison other frogs, it should be housed alone.

Breedability: Fairly easy.

Keeping Requirements: One 10-gallon "half and half" aquaterrarium, with warm pond and soft, moist substrate. Most importantly, it can only be kept with others of its species.

Miscellaneous Facts: The Pickerel Frog is one of the most handsome of all anurans. Its pleasing shades of brown and tan make it a very attractive pet. Although fairly common in the wild, it will not hesitate to make way from the nearest water source upon sensing danger. Because of a potent skin excretion it cannot be housed with other species of frogs and toads.

Fire-bellied Toad
Bombina orientalis

Description: Brilliant green base color on back with a large peppering of

The Pickerel Frog, *Rana palustris*, is a beautiful animal and does well in captivity, but should only be housed with others of the same species. Due to the toxic nature of its skin, it will harm frogs and toads of different species. Photo by R. T. Zappalorti.

One of the most popular anurans in the pet hobby is the Fire-bellied Toad, *Bombina orientalis*. This attractive little creature is highly aquatic and has an even temper, and usually is sold at a relatively affordable price. Photos by (top) W. Mudrack and (bottom) B. Kahl.

dark spots. Belly also covered with miscellaneous spotting, but belly color is bright red or orange, hence the common name.

Geographical Range: Eastern Siberia, and parts of China and Korea.

Natural Habitat:

plant cover.

Miscellaneous Facts: Like many other anurans, the Fire-bellied Toad has a toxic secretion on its skin which it uses against predators. It also has an interesting defensive stance which involves the specimen showing its

There are few anurans more bizarre looking than the Surinam Toad, *Pipa pipa*. A native of South American waters, it is totally aquatic and takes a wide variety of food items. Photo by W. P. Mara.

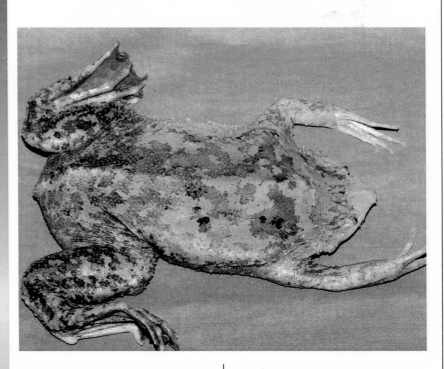

Mountain streams.

Temperament: Jumpy. Not nasty, but very active.

Diet: Insects, etc.

Response To Captivity: Favorable. A very hardy animal.

Breedability: Fairly easy.

Keeping Requirements: Respectable amount of water; reasonably warm. Soft substrate. Prefers

bright underside (which is usually a brilliant orange or red color, thus the common name). In the last few years, this animal has become a very popular and widely available pet.

Surinam Toad
  Pipa pipa
  Description: Unique in shape—slightly elongated, flattened body (usually

ashy gray to dirty tan), with a highly distinctive arrow-shaped head, the point being the snout.

Geographical Range: South America.

Natural Habitat: Aquatic.

Temperament: Nervous, but adaptable.

The Surinam Toad has fascinated hobbyists for many years, but has only recently been kept as a pet. Its moderate temper and steady eating habits are legendary. Although somewhat odd-looking, it is nevertheless somehow quite attractive.

The Spring Peeper, *Pseudacris crucifer,* is one of the tiniest frogs in the eastern United States. A resident of wet woodland areas, it feeds on small insects and does fairly well in captivity. Photo by W. Mudrack.

Diet: Fish, liver, beef heart, worms, shrimp, etc.

Response To Captivity: Very well.

Breedability: Fairly simple.

Keeping Requirements: Warm water tank, sandy substrate, and a few secure hiding spots. A varied diet for peak health.

Miscellaneous Facts:

Spring Peeper
Pseudacris crucifer
Description: Very small. Colors can be tan, gray, or brown, and there is a distinctive dark "X"-shaped mark on the back. Toe pads are very prominent.

Geographical Range: Found all across the eastern half of the United States, and north into Canada.

Natural Habitat: Woodlands near swamps, lakes, ponds, etc.

Temperament: Calm, but alert. Spends much time clung to leaves, branches, etc.; i.e., under cover.

Diet: Insects, etc.

Response To Captivity: Fairly hardy, but must have privacy.

Breedability: Somewhat difficult. Likes to breed during warm rains. Not recommended for beginners.

Keeping Requirements: A moist, slightly humid tank with much plant cover.

Miscellaneous Facts: Although known for its distinctive trilling on warm spring nights, the Spring Peeper is rarely *seen*. Capable of blending almost translucently into its background, it will cling to the surface of trees, plants, and aquatic grasses, without a sound until all dangers pass by. Although they make hardy pets, they will hide so much that you probably won't get the chance to see them.

Pine Barrens Treefrog
Hyla andersoni

Description: Brilliant green back with a distinct purple stripe down each side, and two copper-colored eyes.

Geographical Range: Scattered populations in southern New Jersey, the Carolinas, Florida (panhandle), and southeastern Alabama.

Natural Habitat: Swamps, bogs, ponds, lakes, etc. Muddier areas.

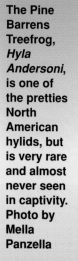

The Pine Barrens Treefrog, *Hyla Andersoni*, is one of the pretties North American hylids, but is very rare and almost never seen in captivity. Photo by Mella Panzella

Temperament: Calm, even-tempered.

Diet: Insects, etc.

Response To Captivity: Fair at best.

Breedability: Easy.

Keeping Requirements: Moisture (especially in the substrate), plants, branches.

Miscellaneous Facts: Somewhat hard to acquire legally, the Pine Barrens Treefrog only makes a fair pet at best, mainly because, unlike others of its genus, it is not an aggressive eater. Thus, the keeper has to provide it with very small food items and house it alone (i.e., not with other, more aggressive, frog species). This is a shame, for it is a remarkably attractive animal.

Colorado River Toad
Bufo alvarius
Description: Heavy, stocky body. Very large, especially for a North American anuran—up to 7.5 in/19 cm. Olive or dark brown, with smooth skin.

Geographical Range: extreme southwest Arizona, southern New Mexico, some parts of extreme southeast California (and just into Baja California), then into Mexico.

Natural Habitat: Damp desert regions, although sometimes found in grasslands.

Temperament: Very calm, but will snap at your fingers if you get them too close (and the bites are quite painful).

Diet: Seemingly

One of the hardiest anurans, not to mention one of the most intelligent, is the Colorado River Toad, *Bufo alvarius*. Photo by Jon W. Church

anything. Insects, worms, small mice, other amphibians, etc.

Response To Captivity: Does very well in captivity.

Breedability: Easy.

Keeping Requirements: Needs a large water pool, a varied diet, and a dry, sandy area to retreat to.

Miscellaneous Facts: The Colorado River Toad is one of the most intelligent of all anurans and will eat right from your hand, but be careful—it also has a tendency to snap, thus possibly nipping off pieces of your skin in the process. It is very hardy and does extremely well in captivity, although specimens are getting harder and harder to acquire commercially. It is active mostly at night.

Mexican Burrowing Toad
Rhinophrynus dorsalis
Description: Fat, bulbous body, with tiny eyes. Coloration is usually dark (gray to brown) with a distinct broad stripe running down the back (yellow, red, or orange). The head is pointed and narrow and the skin in fairly smooth.

Geographical Range: Only found in the southernmost tip of Texas in the United States, then south through Mexico to Costa Rica.

Natural Habitat: Soft, cultivated areas.

Temperament: Calm but careful. Easily angered.

Diet: Primarily termites.

A rare sight—a pair of Mexican Burrowing Toads. *Rhinophrynus dorsalis*, locked in amplexus. Photo by R. T. Zappalorti

Keep Couch's Spadefoot Toad, *Scaphiopus couchi*, in a dry, desert-type terrarium and sustain it on a diet of crickets and spiders. This is one of the handsomest species in the United States. Photo by Ken Lucas.

Response To Captivity: So-so. Likes to bury itself, so it probably won't be seen too often. Only active during night hours, and has a particular diet, which may or may not be easy to obtain depending on the keeper's means.

Breedability: Somewhat difficult. It seems to only breed in pools created by warm rainfall.

Keeping Requirements: A thick layer of soft, loamy soil for burrowing purposes.

Miscellaneous Facts: The Mexican Burrowing Toad is a strange creature, and the only member of its genus to be found in the United States. When angered, it will blow itself up like a balloon; a tactic is also occasionally used as a means of buoyancy for swimming.

Couch's Spadefoot Toad
Scaphiopus couchi
Description: Small (under 3.5 in/8.9 cm) and very attractive. Yellow and black (or dark gray) intermittent "net" pattern on back and a notable curved "spade" on each hind foot, hence the common name.

Geographical Range: Extreme southwestern parts of the U.S. (only the southernmost parts of California), into Baja California, and Mexico.

Natural Habitat: Drier terrain—mesquite, creole, prairies, etc.

Temperament: Calm.

Diet: Insects, small lizards, spiders, etc.

Response To Captivity: Fairly hardy, but must have dry surroundings.

Breedability: Somewhat difficult. Mates in pools after heavy rainstorms.

The Eastern Narrow-mouthed Frog, *Gastrophryne carolinensis*, will require an aqua-terrarium setup with a loose soil substrate. Some specimens may take crickets and spiders, but most prefer ants. Photo by R. D. Bartlett.

Keeping Requirements: Small water pool; a cool, dark, hiding place; the rest of the tank should be dry. Sand is the choice bedding, and should be deep.

Miscellaneous Facts: Most of the Spadefoots make decent pets, but breeding them is more or less a challenge best left to the pros. This is one frog that is almost never seen commercially, which is sad because it is beautiful.

Eastern Narrow-mouthed Frog
Gastrophryne carolinensis

Description: Plump and very small (under 2 in/5 cm), with a brilliant orange and black pattern on the back, and a grayish belly. A distinctive fold of skin across the back of the head.

Geographical Range: Most of the southeastern quarter of the U.S.

Natural Habitat: Never far from water. Grassy, quiet areas. Will also not stray far from loose vegetation or soil.

Temperament: Jumpy, nervous.

Diet: Prefers ants but will also eat different types of insects and spiders.

Response To Captivity: Hardy, but prefers privacy.

Breedability: Easy, but eggs are somewhat delicate.

Keeping Requirements: A fair amount of humidity, a large pool, and some plants, both aquatic and terrestrial. Also, a thick layer of

One of the most primitive of all frogs, the Tailed Frog, *Ascaphus truei*, gets its name from the fact that the tail it has during its tadpole stage does not get fully absorbed in adulthood. Photo by David Green.

warm, loose soil in which to hide.

Miscellaneous Facts: This is one of the more attractive and underrated frogs. It is not seen in pet stores too often, but adapts to human company over time and seems to thrive in captivity as long as it is left alone (i.e., it will become stressed if exposed for long periods). It is also nocturnal, but occasionally can be seen foraging during daylight hours.

Tailed Frog

Ascaphus truei

Description: Small (under 2 in/5 cm), with a beautiful honey-golden coloration spotted by black or dark brown. The males have an oblong "tail" (thus the name) used for breeding purposes.

Geographical Range: Very limited. Only found in parts of southern British Colombia, and in the northwestern corner of the United States.

Natural Habitat: Colder areas. Mountain streams, wet woodlands, etc.

Temperament: Nervous.

Diet: Algae, very small vertebrates, other tadpoles. Some insects, but not a top preference.

Response To Captivity: Fairly good. Not particularly hard to keep, but rarely, if ever, seen in captivity.

Breedability: Difficult.

The largest anuran in the United States, the Bullfrog, *Rana catesbeiana*, can grow to over 8 in/20 cm. It needs plenty of space in captivity and will accept a wide variety of food items, including smaller frogs and toads, so be careful who you house it with. Photo by Mella Panzella.

Keeping Requirements: A cold aquatic tank, with running water.

Miscellaneous Facts: This is one of the most primitive of all anurans. It still has vestigial muscles that enable it to move its "tail" about, and no vocal ability whatsoever.

Bullfrog

Rana catesbeiana

Description: The largest frog in North America, occasionally reaching over 8 in/20 cm. Emerald or drab green upper body, becoming browner near hind region. Belly whitish, and the head boasts distinctly large eardrum.

Geographical Range: Most of the eastern half of the U.S., and only sparsely scattered through the western half, except along the extreme west coast, where it is abundant.

Natural Habitat: Exclusively prefers aquatic surroundings. Will not stray from ponds, lakes, etc.

Temperament: Nervous and alert.

Diet: Frogs, fish, crayfish, large insects. Has been known to grab snakes, newborn turtles, mice, and even small birds.

Response To Captivity: Does well, but must be given time to adapt to human company.

Breedability: Moderate. Requires large water masses and plant life.

Keeping Requirements: A very large tank, mostly

A handsome and generally overlooked creature, the Carpenter Frog, *Rana virgatipes,* does very well in captivity, feeding on a variety of insects and breeding willingly. It prefers a tank with plenty of plant cover, and thus may not be seen as often as a keeper might wish. Photo by R. T. Zappalorti.

water. Small land areas should be muddy (or moist at least) and with a large degree of aquatic plant cover.

Miscellaneous Facts: The Bullfrog is a very hardy fellow, as well as being quite stout and handsome. Its croak is notorious in the wilderness (a very deep, guttural "jug-o-rum") as well as its tendency to jump at the nearest sign of danger. They are very hard to capture.

Carpenter Frog
Rana virgatipes
Description: Four yellowish stripes down back, but lacking in dorsolateral folds. Reasonably small (under 3 in/7.5 cm). Olive-gray to medium brown base color.

Geographical Range: Lower half of the U.S.

east coast.

Natural Habitat: Sphagnum bogs and fringes. Also, areas with dense vegetation and slow-moving streams.

Temperament: Jumpy and alert.

Diet: Insects, etc.

Response To Captivity: Does well; very hardy.

Breedability: Fairly easy.

Keeping Requirements: Large pool, moist land masses. Prefers plant cover for security.

Miscellaneous Facts: Although a nervous little frog, the Carpenter is adaptable to captivity and seems to prefer the company of other frogs. In the wild, it will dart into the nearest body of water when disturbed, but then shows its head only seconds later apparently to "check out" its pursuer.

Shown are an adult pair of Carpenter Frogs, *Rana virgatipes*, at a breeding pond. The male, above, is in mid-call. Photo by R. T. Zappalorti.

Brimley's Chorus Frog
Pseudacris brimleyi
Description: Very small (rarely over an 1 in/2.5 cm), with a set of medium brown stripes running laterally (through eye on downward) along a tan-colored back.
Geographical Range: Coastal Plain regions of Virginia, the Carolinas, and Georgia.
Natural Habitat: Marshy, boggy areas, with only moderate vegetation and plant matter.
Temperament: Fairly calm, but objects to handling.
Diet: Various insects.
Response To Captivity: Fairly easy to keep.
Breedability: Unknown.
Keeping Requirements: Standard paludarium setup.
Miscellaneous Facts: A

Notice the distinct light striping down the back of the Carpenter Frog, *Rana virgatipes*. That, plus the lack of a dorsolateral fold, characterizes the species. Photo by Mella Panzella.

Abundant in many locales, Fowler's Toad, *Bufo woodhousei fowleri*, does well in captivity, but be careful when picking them up—they may empty out their cloacal contents in your hand! They prefer a diet of crickets and spiders (and tinier anurans, so beware), and a loose, sandy substrate in which to burrow. Photo by Mella Panzella.

Rarely growing over 1 in/ 2.5 cm, Brimley's Chorus Frog, *Pseudacris brimleyi*, can be found in the southeastern United States, where it haunts marshes and bogs during the night hours in search of tiny insects. Photo by R. D. Bartlett.

very attractive frog, but not often seen, even in the wild. This is not so much due to its wanting to hide as the simple fact that it's so tiny. It also has the ability to change color quite fast, thus efficiently hiding itself from predators.

Woodhouse's Toad
Bufo woodhousei
Description: Plump and moderate in size (up to 5 in/12.5 cm). Skin mottled and warty, with a gray base color flecked in black.

Geographical Range: Widespread across the U.S. although not as common in the extreme west or near the Great Lakes.

Natural Habitat: Sandy, but occurs in some damp

areas, i.e., pools created by rainfall.

Temperament: Nervous.
Diet: Insects.
Response To Captivity: Does well. Primarily nocturnal.

Breedability: Easy.
Keeping Requirements: Sand, with a small degree of moisture, and a fairly large pool, as they like to swim occasionally and are quite good at it.

Miscellaneous Facts: This is one of the more common of all North American toads. It is quite abundant in the wild, and easy to maintain in captivity. Mothers give birth to fairly respectable-sized egg masses, and the eggs transform rather quickly, which is of course a favorable factor for the preservation of the species in the wild. They are also somewhat communal and prefer the company of their own kind, although some of the larger adults will readily consume the younger ones if left hungry enough.

Green Frog
Rana clamitans
Description: A medium-sized frog with a prominent and simple greenish coloring. Like the Bullfrog, it has a large, obvious tympanum.

Geographical Range: Covers much of the eastern half of the United States.

Natural Habitat: Likes to stay near water but can be found in damper woodland areas and under fallen and decaying trees.

Temperament: Fairly tame, even in the wild, but will seek cover if it feels seriously threatened. Comparatively speaking, probably one of the most "laid back" of all aquatic frogs.

Diet: Insects, spiders, other tadpoles, etc.

Response To Captivity: Very hardy.

Breedability: Easy.

Keeping Requirements: A warm body of water, and some plants. Also needs humidity, and a small amount of moisture.

Miscellaneous Facts:

Another easy-to-keep anuran, the Green Frog, *Rana clamitans*, is very calm and relaxed by nature. Some people claim to have walked right up and touched specimens in the wild. Photo by David Green.

The Bronze Frog is an excellent pet, and can be found in pet stores from time to time. A superb first frog for any keeper.

African Clawed Frog

Xenopus laevis

Description: A plump, moderate-sized aquatic frog with a flat, smooth, pear-shaped body and two clawed front legs, with distinct webbed feet in the back. Dirty gray in coloring, but sometimes with brownish tints.

Geographical Range: Primarily from Africa, but colonies have now been introduced into California waters (although it is believed these populations are dying out).

Natural Habitat: Warm, quiet waters.

Temperament: Calm.

Diet: Brine shrimp, various commercial fish foods, etc. They are very scavangerish and will grab basically anything they can get into their mouths.

Response To Captivity: Very hardy and long-lived.

Breedability: Fairly easy. Tadpoles hatch within two full days.

Keeping Requirements: A warm fishtank with hiding places.

Miscellaneous Facts: The African Clawed Frog, once literally unknown to the pet industry, has now become one of the most popular pets of all. Its worry-free keeping requirements coupled with its unique appearance make it a very desirable pet (it is also relatively inexpensive). Even an albino strain is now commonly offered. If a keeper is interested in totally aquatic anurans, then this one is worth checking out.

When dealing with African Clawed Frogs, *Xenopus laevis*, it is best to treat them as you would fish and use a fish-catching net. African Clawed Frogs are very slippery and should not be grabbed by hand. Photo by Isabelle Francais, courtesy of Mark B. Robertson.

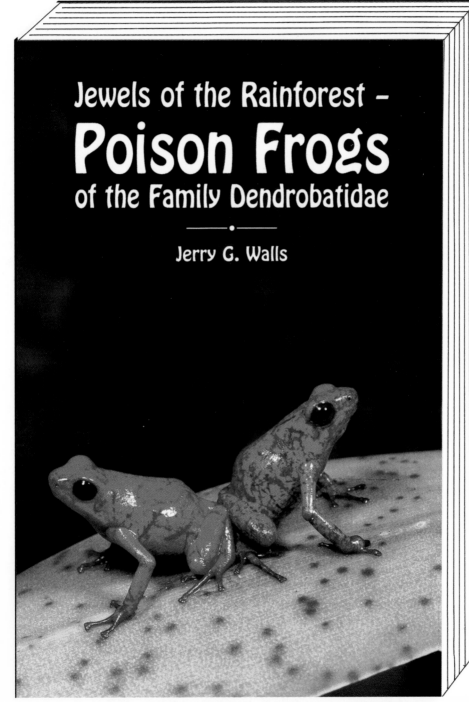

Jewels of the Rainforest –
Poison Frogs
of the Family Dendrobatidae

———•———

Jerry G. Walls

This 288 page, 10X14" volume (TS-223) is the first attempt at a thorough coverage of the brilliantly-colored tropical American poison frogs so popular with advanced hobbyists. For the first time, all species of these little frogs are covered in detail and illustrated withover 500 color photos, over 80 color paintings, and 65 range maps.

Suggested Reading

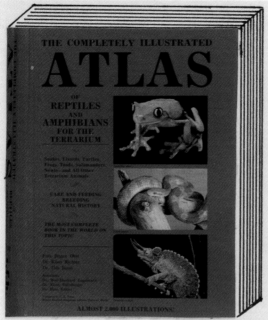

H-1102, 830 pages, Over 1800 color photos

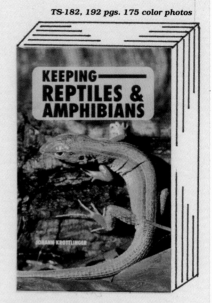

TS-182, 192 pgs. 175 color photos

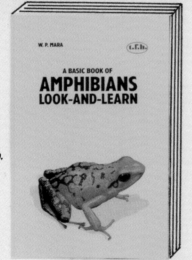

KD-006
(hard cover),
KD-006S
(soft cover
64 pages
230 color
photos

PS-876, 384
pages, 175
color photos

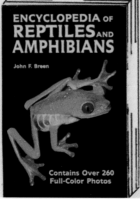

H-935, 576
pages, 260
color photos

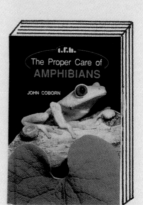

TW-116, 256 pages,
167 color photos

INDEX

Page numbers in **boldface** refer to illustrations.